Fast, Easy & Accurate Router Jigs

Pat Warner

POPULAR WOODWORKING BOOKS
CINCINNATI, OHIO
www.popularwoodworking.com

This book is dedicated to
my son, Derek George Warner.

DISCLAIMER

To prevent accidents, keep safety in mind while you work. Use the safety guards installed on power equipment; they are for your protection. When working on power equipment, keep fingers away from saw blades, wear safety goggles to prevent injuries from flying wood chips and sawdust, wear headphones to protect your hearing, and consider installing a dust vacuum to reduce the amount of airborne sawdust in your woodshop. Don't wear loose clothing, such as neckties or shirts with loose sleeves, or jewelry, such as rings, necklaces or bracelets, when working on power equipment, and tie back long hair to prevent it from getting caught in your equipment. People who are sensitive to certain chemicals should check the chemical content of any product before using it. The author and editors who compiled this book have tried to make all the contents as accurate and correct as possible. Plans, illustrations, photographs and text have been carefully checked. All instructions, plans and projects should be carefully read, studied and understood before beginning construction. Due to the variability of local conditions, construction materials, skill levels, etc., neither the author nor Popular Woodworking Books assumes any responsibility for any accidents, injuries, damages or other losses incurred resulting from the material presented in this book.

07   06   05   04   03   8   7   6   5

Library of Congress Cataloging-in-Publication Data

Warner, Pat.
    Fast, easy and accurate router jigs / by Pat Warner.—1st ed.
       p.   cm.
    Includes index.
    ISBN 1-55870-486-8 (alk. paper)
    1. Routers (Tools)   2. Jigs and fixtures—Design and construction.
3. Woodwork.   I. Title.
TT203.5.W36   1999
684'.08—dc21   99-21734
                           CIP

Edited by R. Adam Blake, Michael Berger, Jeff Crump, Bruce E. Stoker
Designed by Mary Barnes Clark
Cover Photography by Joe Harrison/JH Photography
Computer Illustrations by Eric Johnson
Illustrations by Terry Kirkpatrick

Metric Conversion Chart		
TO CONVERT	TO	MULTIPLY BY
Inches	Centimeters	2.54
Centimeters	Inches	0.4

ACKNOWLEDGMENTS

May I thank the following thoughtful, energetic and skilled people for their part in making this book a success. J.A. Warner, Jürgen Amtmann, Chuck Hicks of Whiteside Machinery Co., Col. Joe Kirkpatrick for his support, Brian Corbley of Amana Tool Corp., Carlo Venditto of Jesada Tools, Jane Howard and Gene Smith of Adjustable Clamp Co., Rich Rapuano of DeWalt Tools, Mike Whitman from Porter-Cable, Chris Carlson of Stanley-Bosch, Barry Rundstrom of PRC, Patrick Spielman, David Arkin M.D., Frank Kunkel, M.D., Gil Boswell, M.D., John Goff, Gary Rogowski, noted singer and jig-master Sandor Nagyszalanczy, Strother Purdy, Dida Warner, Nathan D. Warner, Ross Smith, Dave Keller, Joe Marmo, Mike Mangan of Sears/Craftsman, Mike Roten, Richard Wedler of Microfence, Al & Joan Weiss, Nan Bushley, Tom Clark of *Woodshop News*, Bridge City Tools, Dick Erickson, Russ Filbeck, Chuck Masters, Jerry Funk, Chuck Delaney from Medite, John Ferrie of Ridge Carbide, Jim Tolpin, Curtis Wilson, M.D., John Lavine of *Woodwork Magazine*, and Terry Kirkpatrick for the drawings in chapter nine.

A special thanks to my illustrator, Eric Johnson, who always went above and beyond the call of duty to produce all the drawings in the text.

I am the photographer but shooting film is only half the product. My printer Ken Schroeder is responsible for the other half. His excellent advice and attention to the focus of the composition are, as usual, outstanding.

ABOUT THE AUTHOR

The clay sculptor has the ideal opportunity to contend with any of his mistakes. The malleability of his material allows for an infinite number of remedies at little expense or risk to the project. The woodworker, on the other hand, has only two choices when presented with an error. He can make the workpiece over or change the work to suit the mishap; both options are likely to involve compromise. The key, then, is getting it right the first time.

My nature is to make mistakes. I'm not one to get it right on the first go-around. Notwithstanding, if I do it more than once I usually do it better each time. Twenty-three years of self-taught woodworking has been one long series of mistakes. However, since I've screwed up so many times in so many ways I've become pretty good at what I do.

My education was in the sciences and therefore I have learned and I've been blessed with excellent observational skills. This combination of hands-on experience and a keen sense of the task makes it easy for me to know when something is apt to go wrong. When I'm in uncharted territory I'm only half as likely to blow it.

As a furniture designer/craftsman I've designed and made hundreds of pieces. I'm skilled in case goods and sleepware, and I'm no stranger to benches, desks, tables and seating. I've made all my jigs and fixtures and I've made a few on commission. My primary tool has been and still is the router. I use a dozen or so for ordinary work, and I often apply them to tasks most woodworkers would find strange or at the very least serendipitous. I do all my joinery with routers, I joint all stock edges on one, and, of course, all my template and pattern work is router cut.

I've been called on by the router bit and router manufacturing industry to consult from time to time, and I teach routing at the Palomar Community College in San Marcos, California. I am the inventor of the Acrylic Offset Router Sub-Base, and I make the accessory for the Porter-Cable Corporation. Incidentally my subbase is hand fabricated with an assortment of twin-pin, table and hand routers using seven different cutters.

This is my third book on routing for Popular Woodworking Books, and I have authored some 60 articles on routing and making furniture with routers.

Look for my book on *Templates and Routing* coming soon, and visit my Web site, www.patwarner.com.

TABLE OF CONTENTS

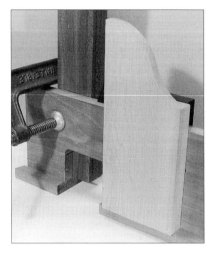

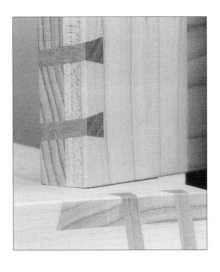

TABLE OF CONTENTS

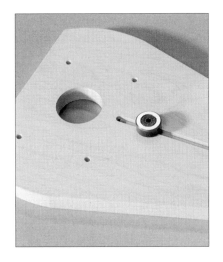

INTRODUCTION

Woodworking machines and hand cutting tools need jigs and fixtures to facilitate their full capabilities. A table saw can slice up wood nicely but tenon making requires a fixture. You can plane your stock to uniform thickness from end to end, but if you want your work to taper you've got to fixture it. Drilling holes in line on the drill press requires a fence. Band sawing circles can be done free hand, but if you want two of them with the same diameter you'll need a jig to do it. For me, hand tools are just as dependent on jigs. I can't even steer a corner chisel into the corner of a mortise without a guide. I've seen lots of shooting boards in the British publications, so I think they may have a little trouble "following the line," too. The point is, most cutting tools need assistance to carry out their assigned duties and routers are the worst case scenario; they're simply helpless and in need of assistance.

I am surprised that the solutions to getting control of the router are easy. Intuitively, you wouldn't think a spinning tool enshrined in a metal casting would lend itself to fixturing and jigging so well, but it does. On first inspection some of the jigs in this book may look sophisticated, but I can I assure you it's just an illusion. The use of machine bolts instead of toilet bolts, levers instead of epoxied turnings on all-thread, and fiberboard instead of particleboard is really all that separates my paraphernalia from the "one-off" jigs so often found in the literature. Neatness also counts some, but, since I've made my jigs many times over and simplified them, they're fundamentally straightforward and require only average woodworking skills to make.

I would like to point out a peculiarity I've discovered while making and improving jigs. It often takes the jig itself to make the jig, and, without a good working model to begin with, the first generation of the jig is usually unsweet. For example, it takes a router fence (chapter twelve) to make a router fence, and, oddly enough, the tenoner (chapter nine) can be used as a platform with a pair of edge guides (chapter six) and a plunge router to make the sliding stops for the mortiser (chapter eleven)! Consequently, as each jig is rebuilt, the next generation is much sweeter than its predecessor.

As this evolution transpires, your work improves, and you'll often find more uses for the same jig. Moreover, with a constellation of jigs such as mine, you'll be making improvements only made practical with the jigs themselves. You might discover that in my book there is no definition for a jig or fixture. The machinists have their definition, the mechanical engineers and woodworkers have another. Some say a jig is for guiding the tool, some say it's for holding the work. Fixtures are said to secure and index the work while remaining fixed. Some of the tools in my list secure and index the work and are themselves the reference for the router to make the cut—and they move! For me, the pursuit of their definitions is silly. Why not improve your woodworking and routing skills instead? Make jig-fixtures; don't worry, be happy.

CHAPTER ONE
Routers and Jigs

Figure 1-1
Routers need a lot of stuff to make themselves useful.

In order for us furniture/cabinet makers to be in control of both the design and production of our woodwork, we need tools. For example, a jointer and planer give us command of thickness and squareness. The table and radial saws chop our boards or panels both parallel and to the correct length. The band saw is a marvelous accessory to rough-cut our stock, and it's essential to cutting curvy lines. Sanders take bandsawn material closer to a finished state, and if they're well fixtured, they can produce precision parts. There is no substitute for a drill press when it comes to boring holes and other secondary drilling operations such as tapping, chamfering or countersinking. Hand tools, both electric and people-powered, are as important as the stationaries and, in some cases, can substitute for them.

In general, stationary tools and many hand tools are ready for work once they're plugged in or sharpened. The table saw has its miter gauge, fence and tilting arbor assembly. Tension the blade, align the guides, hit the switch and the band saw is at the ready. The sander and drill press are pretty much self-evident, too. The jigsaw has few, if any, useful accessories. Ditto for the hand drill/driver, orbital sander, grinder, circular saw, flashlight or vacuum cleaner. But enter the router, and "woe betide."

More accessory stuff is required for the router than for any other tool. It needs special bearings, cutters, collars, collets, subbases, fences, wrenches, guides, templates, tables and, most importantly, jigs and fixtures to do anything at all (Figure 1-1).

A router is raw simplicity—a very high-speed, power-hungry motor with a tool holder (collet) on the end of its armature. It's up to you to make it useful. There are only two types of

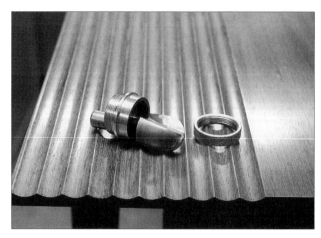

Figure 1-3
The flutes in this table were produced from a straight template, collar and 1" core box bit (shown). I moved the template ⅝" for each cut.

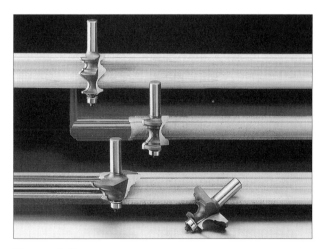

Figure 1-2
This grouping of molding cutters is typical of the kind of bearing/edge-guided tools available for simple decoration. These cuttings can, for the most part, be accomplished without any fixturing. (Photo supplied by Amana Tool.)

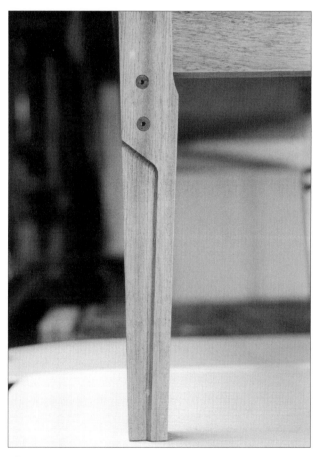

Figure 1-4
This decorative cut was defined by a template with the same shape. The cut does not follow the edge of the leg.

Figure 1-5
The template jig used in Figure 1-4 is shown here with its toggle clamps and a Jesada Tools cutter. The router does its work on the uncluttered opposite face of the jig.

routers (plunge and fixed-base), though there are at least 75 different models to choose from. For this book, one plunge router and at least one fixed-base router will be required to use the jigs and fixtures and, in some cases, to make them. In my first two books, *Getting the Very Best From Your Router* and *The Router Joinery Handbook*, I use a lot of ink to describe just what makes a good router and what you can do with one. Let me take a moment to condense some of that information which, in turn, may help you better understand the origin and design of my jigs and fixtures.

Routers are very intrusive. You can, with the appropriate equipment, decorate, cut joints and mill. The decorative cuttings are largely created from bearing-piloted cutters zingin' down the edges of stock (Figures 1-2, 1-3, 1-4, 1-5). With the assistance of templates, the cutter pathway can be ever changing and more interesting, even on straight edges (Figure 1-3). There are hundreds of decorative cutters, and combinations of them used at different depths of cut often produce very striking results. The usual method of embellishment, however, is with a fixed-base

Figure 1-6
These joints were all cut with shop-made jigs and fixtures.

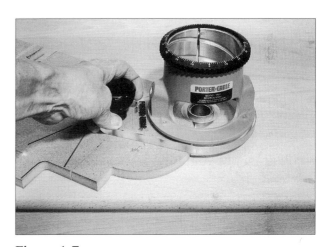

Figure 1-7
The router and its offset subbase accessory improve ordinary routings, but they're especially valuable at the ends of the work and turning 90° corners.

router in hand, with one bearing-guided cutter, at one depth, or off the fence on the router table. Since these cuttings are so trivial, there are few jigs that simplify their use.

Millwork, in this instance, refers to those cuttings that are not joinery and not decorative. These cuttings could be rounding stock for dowels, square-corner notching, jointing, making circles and templates. There are a lot of other milling operations, but these particular processes can be facilitated with the jigs and fixtures in the chapters that follow.

The router is king when it comes to cutting joints. No other single tool has its prowess. Tongues, grooves, laps, mortises and tenons, dovetails, glue joints, splines, scarfs and box joints can all be cut with routers (Figure 1-6). There are probably more jigs and fixtures for joinery than for any other category of routing. Most of the jigs in this book are for joints, but one could argue that the router table fence—a jig in its own right (see chapter twelve)—can be used for most router operations whether for decorative, joint making or millwork cutting.

No book on router jigs and fixtures is complete without an overview of routers. Allow me to make a few points about them and indicate why a certain tool may have particular advantages over another. Furthermore, to get the most out of my jigs, I'll help you select what I think are the best tools for the job.

PLUNGE OR FIXED-BASE?

Router work can be done on the face, edge or even on the end of a stick. Cuttings can be blind-ended (never cut through to an edge), through, inside or out. Edge cuts (outside) are most frequently done at only one depth. Fixed-base routers work most effectively on the edges of stock because they are centered low and are more stable than plunge routers. With an offset subbase on a fixed-base router, a trip around any corner or curvy line template is a stable one (Figure 1-7). Furthermore, the multidepth mechanisms, so sophisticated on plunge routers, are unnecessary for single-depth cuts. (It's like having cruise control on a car driven only in the city.) Consequently, most of my jigs that are used on outside cuts are done with fixed-base routers.

Inside cuttings and cuts that require multi-depth settings are more suited for the plunge router. And you will notice that if a cutting happens to be multistage (cut at many depths) and outside, provision has been made to totally support the casting of the plunge tool.

In my view, plunge routers have a high center of mass and are less stable than fixed-base tools. Therefore, they perform poorly on outside cuts where there is always less than 45 percent of the base casting footprint on the work. On 90° turns that number falls to less than 23 percent; moreover, you cannot safely plunge a plunge router without all of the casting on terra firma. Attempts to gain back stability with an offset subbase are frustrated because of the wide handle separation and the center of mass that changes constantly with each change in depth. A better strategy, then, is to reserve the outside cuts and cuts along a template edge for the fixed-base router and reserve inside and multi-depth cuts for the plunge router. The choice of router (plunge or fixed-base) for a given jig or fixture and the design of my fixtures themselves are based on these factors.

Figure 1-8
The Porter-Cable 690 and Porter-Cable 42193 off-set subbase are the ideal combination for edge and template single-depth cuttings.

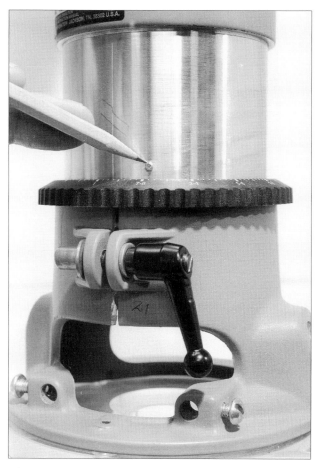

Figure 1-9

The Porter-Cable 690 motor hangs on four pins which engage the twin ground spirals inside the base casting. A 180° clockwise twist of the motor lowers the cutter 1". The motor lock lever has been upgraded.

Figure 1-10

The DeWalt 610 has an offset subbase (DeWalt 6917) which accepts the same size collar guide assembly as the Porter-Cable 690. The rack-and-pinion gear raises the motor more than 2". The lock/lever has been upgraded. The tool is zeroable at any depth.

Figure 1-11

The collet nut has been machined so that it fits into the collar guide, effectively extending the motor travel some ⅜".

Router Selection

Department store routers are satisfactory tools for the limited duty they're assigned to, but their small collets, modest depth of cut range and low horsepower will prove to be a problem. An industrial-grade tool is not that much more expensive, and in today's fierce market competition, industrial tool value has never been greater. Moreover, you'll get a tool that will stand up to the rigors of time and service. And if you lose the desire to do woodworking, you can always sell the tool for more than you'd ever get from the resale of a department store router. Consider buying one or more of the following tools.

Figure 1-12

The Milwaukee 5680 is a 12 amp, 9-pound tool (shown here with my accessory offset subbase). The top is broad and flat, its wire set is indestructible, and its collet is probably the best of all routers. The nut is an octagon that will not fit inside a collar guide.

The Fixed-Base Router

Let's look at six fixed-base designs. Five of the six are fairly evenly matched, performance-wise, but differ slightly in design, weight and power.

The Porter-Cable 690 is by far the most popular industrial router in this class. Porter-Cable supplies an offset subbase as an accessory for this tool (model 42193) which you will find invaluable, and in some cases essential, in using the hand router jigs (Figure 1-8). This 1½ hp, lightweight but powerful tool has plenty of vertical motor travel and very good cutter visibility. It differs from the other tools in its motor-lifting mechanism (Figure 1-9) and its smaller base casting.

The DeWalt 610 is another excellent 1½ hp tool in this class. A variation of this machine has been in production for over 30 years. It too has an accessory offset subbase (DeWalt 6917) that accepts Porter-Cable type collar guides. This router has the advantage of a simple combination rack-and-pinion motor-lift/lock mechanism

Figure 1-13

The Bosch 1604A has been a good tool for years. Its motor is light and powerful (11 amps) and is encased in a durable material, and its collet system never sticks on the cutter.

and the smallest collet nut of the quintet. The small collet nut allows deeper reach into the collar guide, a definite bonus (Figures 1-10, 1-11).

The Milwaukee 5680 is heavier than the other two tools but the most powerful at 2 hp. It is comfortable and, in my view, has the best collet system of all routers. Also, its very flat top facilitates easier cutter changes. Its motor-lift mechanism is of the ring-hung type. The threaded motor casting engages a plastic ring that rests on the base casting. Turn it clockwise the motor rises. Its smooth acting lift is accurate, but it is not zeroable. Milwaukee offers no offset subbase for this tool, but you can get a completely machined one from the author (see Sources and Figure 1-12).

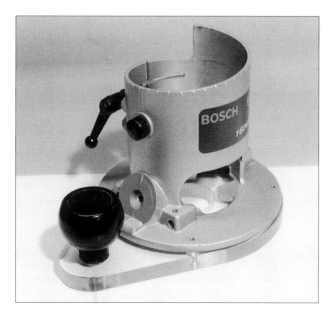

Figure 1-14
The 1604A casting (shown here with my accessory offset subbase) is terminated in a graceful 1" helical rise. The 1604 was the first domestic fixed-base router with a dust extraction accessory.

The final entries in this category are the Bosch 1604A and 1617EVS. The 1604A, at 1¾ hp, is very powerful and spry. Its unusual motor-lift system is not zeroable but has the advantage of zero backlash, a real plus when changing depth by small amounts. The base casting is light and feminine with a 1" helix rise cast into its upper torso (Figure 1-13). A projection on the motor slides up and down the ramp (helix) with the utmost simplicity. Depths of cut are therefore restricted to about 1". Bosch S/B Power Tools does not supply an offset subbase accessory for this tool, but one is available from me, completely machined, with a cutter hole ready to accept Porter-Cable collar guides (Figure 1-14).

The Bosch 1617EVS has recently been introduced to replace the 1604. This new tool (not shown) has been tested by the author and is so promising it may take the lead in this class of routers.

There are many more fixed-base tools, but, as

Figure 1-15
The Porter-Cable 7518 is essentially in a class by itself. It's a heavy tool, but that weight can absorb a cutter error or kickback without much ado. While smaller routers can steer off erratically in the event of a cutter accident, the 7518 is a steamroller. This router is my first choice for the router table and all heavy-duty sustained hand cuts. The 7518 motor barrel is the longest in the industry. If you can't "reach it" with this tool, you won't reach it.

of this writing, it is my opinion that you will be hard pressed to buy more value or quality than is expressed in these five commercial-grade, midrange power tools.

The Porter-Cable 7518, however, is in a class by itself. It is suitable for router table or handheld use. The other fixed-base tools would be overworked in the router table. (An offset sub-

Figure 1-16
The DeWalt 621 is a splendid, light, powerful plunge router. It's the first to have vacuum cleanup built right into the tool.

base is offered by Porter-Cable, model 42194, for this tool.) The tool is available as a variable speed, model 7518, or single speed, 7519. Both tools are soft start, while, with the exception of the Bosch 1617EVS, none of the previously mentioned tools are. If for any reason you're unhappy with the power output or duty of the smaller fixed-base tools, you will not be dissatisfied with this one. This 14½ pounder has more vertical motor travel than any fixed-base and most plunge routers (Figure 1-15).

Router table work is usually full depth, single pass, and against the cutter rotation. As such the power demand is high. For this and many other reasons the Porter-Cable 7518 is also my choice for the router table.

The Plunge Router

There are many operations with my jigs and fixtures that can't be done in one pass. Sometimes the cutter flute is simply too short or the power demand too great. In these situations, a plunge router will prove most invaluable. Plunge routers are designed for multistage work, and

Figure 1-17
The DeWalt 625 is often considered the industry standard in plunge routers. Its excellent collet system, powerful soft-start motor and glass-smooth plunging action are hallmarks of good design and engineering.

fortunately the power demand (usually) is relatively modest for each cut. There are a lot of good plunge machines that are powerful and lightweight, such as the Bosch 1613 and the DeWalt 621 (Figure 1-16). The Porter-Cable 693 hybrid is also a good contender. The DeWalt 625 is generally considered the industry leader in the macho class 3 hp area (Figure 1-17). It's one of the oldest.

So, if you want to rout, make and use jigs and fixtures, you should consider a complement of three routers: one medium-weight fixed-base router; the Porter-Cable 7518 (or 7519) for full-range fixed-base or table routing; and an intermediate weight (9 to 11 pounds) plunge router for multistage work.

CHAPTER TWO

What Makes a Good Router Jig or Fixture?

There are some tools that are designed precisely for a specific task; a tap is one, a bicycle chain tool is another. They may still require a certain amount of skill or dexterity, but their focus ensures there can be no mistake about what they do. Other "form-follows-function" tools include bumper jacks, divining rods and corner chisels.

On the other hand, there are tools that are quite general in nature. Sewing needles, hand planes and pick-axes, for example, all perform a variety of jobs within their respective domains. Routers are like this; they are concise and simple in their design. Getting the most out of them, however, requires some practice, knowledge and, most importantly, a battery of jigs and fixtures. It is a fact of woodworking life that jigs and fixtures are critically necessary for high-quality router work. The designs and uses of these fixtures are sometimes not clear, but you have me to help you simplify design and construction. Moreover, virtually all of the jigs and fixtures that follow have already been through enough shop evolution that they're in their simplest form with as few parts as possible. They're ready to perform as advertised. With my jigs and a little afternoon practice, you'll get the experience and knowledge to become a router expert in no time.

Figure 2-1
Here two pieces of MDF are used to trap the miter gauge blade (parallel to the fence) on the router table. You could slot the table easily enough, but for the occasional use of the gauge, what could be simpler?

THE PRINCIPLES OF GOOD FIXTURING

As you make and use my jigs, I'd like you to consider a number of principles. These principles apply not only here but for any tool you're likely to make for whatever task.

Keep It Simple

Simplicity equals safety and speed (Figure 2-1). However, it's not easy to make something that is "simple." Often there are so many competing features and structures that simplicity is not attained until the third, fourth or even the *nth* generation. Building trains, planes and cars are like this: Somebody always has a better idea, especially if that individual rides or operates the contrivance.

I always use the stuff I make, and if I like to use a particular jig or fixture, it must be because it's fun and easy. If it's cumbersome, dangerous, or if I have a negative feeling about it, it probably needs some simplification. This feedback process improves my fixturing while, at the same time, upgrading the quality of my work.

Sometimes a fixture is just too ambitious, and I've tried too hard to consolidate as many process steps as possible into the thing. Once I attempted to make a drilling jig that clamped and indexed the work and provided a means for the drilling. The tool was simply beyond my capabilities as a jig maker, so I subtracted out the indexing and layout functions for another jig. The process became a two-step process, but both steps were easier and more accurate. Consider two jigs if you get in over your head on one.

Precision and Accuracy

Jigs and fixtures exist because they facilitate ordinary woodworking, and sometimes they are essential to a given process. They also offer a measure of safety, but perhaps just as important, they improve our accuracy, precision and consistency. One of the reasons they can do this is because of their capacity to index and hold the work in the same way and in the same place so that the tool that acts on the workpiece does so in a precise and measured way (Figure 2-2). A lot of care must go into the jig for this to happen, however. And in my view, if you're going to

Figure 2-2
This specialized template with clamps holds successive workpieces in the same place. The work is indexed off the fence and the end stop.

Figure 2-3
The plastic and beechwood sample edge guide was a reasonable first approximation. The second generation (maple and ¾"-square section aluminum) is prettier, but the third run is cheaper, works better than the other two and is prettier yet.

spend the time to make the tool (and jigs are tools) in the first place, you might as well make it well.

Make a Model

Sometimes I'll make a simple low-grade edition of the jig just to see if it will work before I get

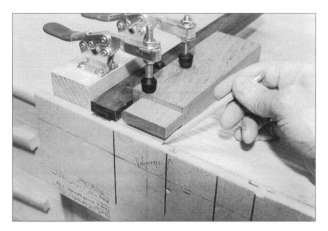

Figure 2-4A
The accuracy of this jig (an experimental tenoner with a screw-driven template) is achieved by first trimming the template parallel to the (oak) work-holding surface.

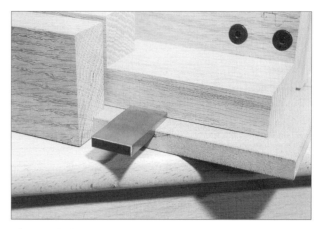

Figure 2-4B
The template in Figure 2-4A travels continuously and parallel to the work because of two steel guides that reside in parallel dadoes perpendicular to the working edge of the template. (This is the back of the jig, upside down.)

involved with the actual working model (Figure 2-3). You should consider this, too, since building anything of quality often casts you into uncharted seas, and you must be good in all the phases of the fabrication to get a good result. Building a test model reveals your deficiencies and gives you an opportunity to do something about them. Jigmaking is a discipline that requires many skills. A piece of woodwork can be made over, reworked or fudged one way or another. A jig has to be right; allow no compromises in safety, accuracy or repeatability (Figures 2-4A, B, C).

Figure 2-4C
This is the reference face of the jig with the steel guides exposed, as the template has been slid to the rear and out of play.

Neatness Counts

The quality of your jigs and fixtures is directly related to the quality of work you put out. While it is possible to get good results from a crummy fixture, more consistent results at faster rates come from jigs that are well made (Figure 2-5). Well-made jigs last longer than crummy ones, but making them requires attention to detail and good layout and measuring tools.

LAYOUT TOOLS

Jigs and fixtures must meet the highest of standards lest anything created from them does not. You can get by with average layout and measuring tools for general woodwork but not with jigs. Here you need control, and precision layout and measuring tools are your keys to it. A stop

Figure 2-5

This jig is the notcher, the subject of chapter four. It isn't reinventing the wheel, but it is a simple well-made tool for a specialized set of cuttings.

Figure 2-6

This ground straightedge is the best tool to set the two halves of my router table fence parallel to one another.

out of square, a reference fence that isn't straight or a mislocated hole all can contribute to inconsistencies.

The Ground Straightedge

Jigmaking starts with a reference edge, and usually every component in the structure has a reference edge, too. The edge must be straight and square. A short 12" to 18" ground straightedge is the best tool to verify straightness, and it's invaluable when it comes to inspecting surfaces for cup, bow, etc. (Figure 2-6).

The Dial Caliper

The dial caliper (Figure 2-7) measures inside, outside and depth. With attachments you can measure the diameter of a hole or its distance to a surface or another hole. A 6" caliper is splendid, but an 8" is even better if you can afford it.

The tool is also critical for measuring results; just how good is your jig? My jigs and fixtures allow you to do accurate and precise wood-

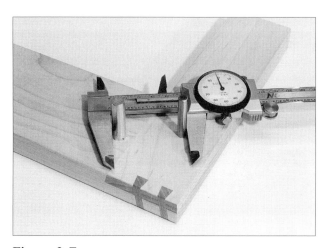

Figure 2-7

You can measure from hole to hole with a dial caliper. The distance from center to center is the measured distance less the sum of the radii of the pins in the holes.

work. Just how well you did cannot be determined with rafter squares and folding rules. The depths of cut, the remaining stock, the thickness or width of your excavations cannot be scrutinized with rough depth gauges or plastic calipers; a precision hardened and ground steel dial caliper is the only practical way to monitor your progress.

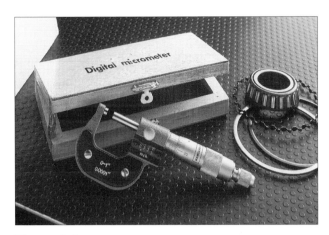

Figure 2-8

There are many ingenious accessories for various depth, inside and pitch measurements, but the "mike" is primarily a simple, inexpensive but very accurate thickness-measuring tool. (Photo supplied by Sears.)

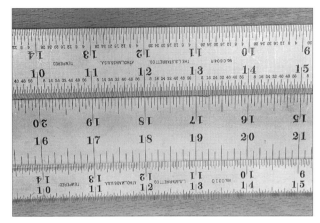

Figure 2-9

These satin-chrome-finished scales can be read in the worst of lighting conditions.

Micrometer

Micrometers are very accurate tools for outside measurements, and there are attachments for them for specialized measurements, too. They come in various ranges, 0 to 1", 1" to 2", etc., but none of them have the capabilities of the dial caliper. If your concern is the cutting result and your measurements fall in the 0 to 2" area, then a "mike" is a good choice (Figure 2-8). It is much cheaper than a dial caliper. Precision tools require care and good storage. If you drop one of these jewels, forever suspect its accuracy.

Scales and Rules

Rules are essential for layout. You should have several. Machinist's quality rules are generally better than woodworking rules, and the scales are more precise and come in many fonts and increments. A 1"- to 1½"-wide rule with a satin finish is easy to read in any light (Figure 2-9). In spite of their precision, each of us will get slightly different measurements because of our own

Figure 2-10

I can't get the same measurement twice from the edge of stock without some sort of reference block as an aid.

optics and the techniques we use to read them. For more consistent readings while measuring from the edge, use a block (see Figure 2-10).

Note that even if you have an accurate rule scaled in 64ths, the best work you can do is on the order of .010" to .020". To work around this, I use stops and fences whenever I can, so all similar operations are referenced by mechanical means rather than a scribed line generated from a rule (Figures 2-11, 2-12).

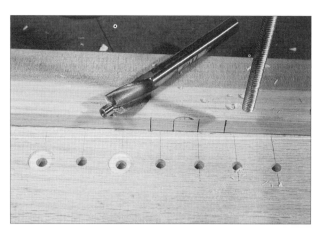

Figure 2-11
All the holes on this board are the same distance from the fence.

Figure 2-12
This photo shows a good example of using a mechanical means to reference work without a scribed line. This indexer is referenced to the jig by the three screws. The work is referenced to the end of the stick that slides in the slot on the indexer, not a scribed line.

The Machinist's Square

Fortunately, a surprising amount of woodworking is done at 90°. It's a good idea, then, to have a machinist's square. Quality squares like the Starrett No. 20 are hardened, made of tool steel, lapped, ground and calibrated. Detective work, such as checking your assembly, can only be verified with well-cared-for precision tools (Figure 2-13). Often each component of your jig and the work produced from it must also be checked for squareness. A square is also handy for setting up machinery. Careful layout, measurement and calibration are essential to good jigmaking. The choice of material is also important. Let's take a minute to explore these choices.

MATERIALS

There are typically four components in my jigs, and each component has its preferred material. The best material does not always wind up in the jig since there are compromises to be made for economy, ease of working the stuff, skills, availability, etc. Nevertheless, the materials in my jigs are time honored and reasonable.

Figure 2-13
The squareness of this jig is not very demanding, but the two panels should be as square as practical without "heroics."

Surface

In a jig there is surface somewhere. The surface can be for mounting components, resting the work or sometimes working the router on

Figures 2-14A&B

In this jig the L-section of oak (above) is for mounting components on, and it's a holding surface for the work. The top of the jig (below) is a template for the hand router.

Figure 2-15

MDF will accept a tap just as well as face-grain wood. The pull strength of a screw in MDF is not as great as wood, but it is good. (About 300 pounds in the face of a ¾"-thick piece.)

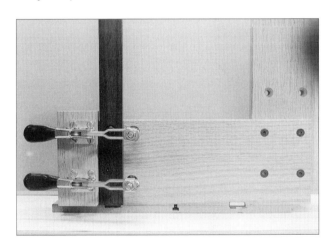

(Figures 2-14A, B). The surface stock should accept fasteners well, drill and machine well, and remain dimensionally stable; cupping and twist are your worst enemies in a router jig. Steel and aluminum are probably the best materials, but I've found medium density fiberboard (MDF) to be one of the best compromises. Plastic, plystock (Baltic birch, plywood, etc.) and wood are more common, but MDF is generally a better choice (Figure 2-15).

Fences and Stops

Fences locate the work on a jig (Figure 2-16). They can also aid in the guidance of a hand tool or the work in the case of router tables. I like wood for fences that locate or index the work. It's easy to make very straight fences out of wood, and it's cheap. Metals are better, but an errant tool bit may be destroyed from an encounter with aluminum, brass or steel. Rosewood, slow-growth walnut, teak and other dense woods are acceptable fence materials. Fences that have to resist abrasion, such as a router table fence, can also be made of wood if they're not too long.

Stops are limiters. They limit travel; they limit position. Stops are essentially insensitive to material. The contact surfaces are usually small, and there is no wear to speak of. Plastic, wood or metal can be used for stops, but whenever possible I use the end grain of hardwood (Figures 2-17, 2-18).

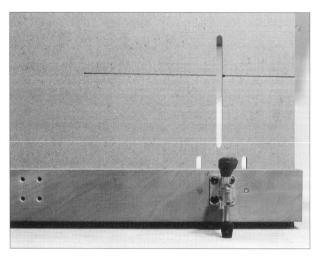

Figure 2-16
By virtue of the slots in the MDF, this fence is adjustable. It is possible to use this jig (with the work on this face) on the table saw with the MDF edge as the guide edge. It is designed for the hand router, however (see similar jig in chapter five).

Figure 2-17
Here I'm using a sliding rosewood stop to locate the work in this prototype lap dovetailer. The end grain is in contact with the work.

Template Stock

There are many occasions when I prefer to fixture the work and rout it with a hand router. In most of these instances, a template—combined with a guide collar or bearing-piloted cutter—is used to facilitate the cut. Once again, MDF is the material of choice for templates. Its edge is not as firm as its face, but it is able to hold fine detail, and it wears satisfactorily. There is some compression of the edge due to the high forces of bearings and guides, but the material is quite good nevertheless. It is intolerant of carbide, however, and if ever your cutter is larger in diameter than its bearing (even by a few thousandths), you will destroy its edge (Figure 2-19).

Hardware

MDF and wood, the primary materials in my jigs, accept wood, sheet metal and machine screws well. Sheet metal screws are stronger (because they are heat treated) than wood

Figure 2-18
The stop in this jig can be positioned in three places. Drilling in three sites for the clamp lever effectively triples its travel. The details of this jig are in chapter four.

screws, and machine screws have more threads per inch than sheet metal or wood screws. I like machine screws. They're made to more exacting standards, and their heads are hard to spoil. The heads and drives I like—the buttonhead, flathead and Allen-drive, respectively—are rare in the other types of screws (Figures 2-20, 2-21).

Figure 2-19

These templates were all ruined by a cutter bigger than its shank bearing. The next time they're used, the bearing may roll on the score and cut another step in the edge. Eventually the whole edge gets wasted.

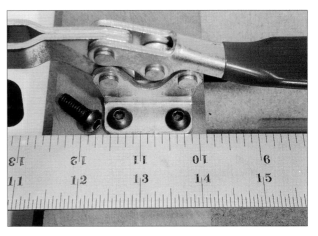

Figure 2-20

These buttonhead machine screws (¼-20) are ideal for holding these toggle clamps in place.

WOOD IN JIGS

Wood is a great material for a lot of things but not as surface stock in jigs and fixtures. There is a strong propensity for its use since, as woodworkers, we have a lot of it. Wood is great for fences and stops, but it's too unstable for a work or reference surface. You can get away with short lengths here and there, and you can use it for prototypes. But if the surface you intend to use it for is much greater than 5" wide or 15" long, don't use it.

I love wood, and I've studied it for a long time. I thought I knew where and how to use it. I was wrong. It warps, it twists, it bows; even if you obey all the rules, it changes shape so often that it's not worth the risk. One router table fence I made had to be jointed every two weeks; it wasted away. I always chose the straightest grain, well seasoned, unstressed, often reglued material. It made no difference. It doesn't distort like an LP record in the sun, but its changes in shape are serious enough that you can't depend on it. You'll notice that the router table fence in chapter twelve is made of wood. The two maple halves are 1"x5"x13". That fence is three years old and still flat and straight. Larger surfaces of wood are not recommended.

Figure 2-21
I polished the head on this 5⁄16-18 socket head cap screw years ago. Wood screws will rust if you spoil their finish.

Besides their durability, I like their machine-shop look, so you'll find them in all of my jigs.

Machine screws require tapping. In this book, I use only ¼-20 and 5⁄16-18. If you'd like to use machine screws, too, drill 13⁄64" holes for the ¼-20 tap and ¼" holes for the 5⁄16-18.

CLAMPING

All jigs and fixtures must capture and hold the work. It is my opinion that once a process has been embodied in a jig, it is an easy matter to clamp the work to the jig. It is important, how-ever, that you trap the work sufficiently, so that a minimum amount of clamping is required (Figure 2-22). If the work is not boxed in, it's easy to dislodge it—even if it has a ton or more of force on it!

I'm sure there will be exceptions, but to date I've always been able to hold the work with C-clamps or toggle clamps. C-clamps always work, but they're not particularly handy, and they require two hands. On the plus side, their load limits are astronomical (1,000 to 10,000 pounds), and they don't bend up the jig (see Figure 2-5).

Toggle clamps, on the other hand, are handy. They're also cheap, capable of high forces, and they act quickly. Their downsides are installa-tion problems, adjustments for different work thicknesses, and they can distort the jig (Figure 2-23). Distortion in a routing jig is your worst enemy. Make sure you don't squeeze the work

Figure 2-22
The work in this mortiser (shown upside down) is trapped by the sliding maple stops and the adjustable jack screws. The end stop not only locates the work but also confines it. See chapter eleven to learn how the mortising jig works.

Figure 2-23
There is so little space beneath the plunger on this toggle clamp that it has to be mounted on a pedestal to hold material thicker than ¾".

so hard that a reference surface starts to bend. The surface of the jig in Figure 2-16 is a refer-ence surface. If you overload the clamps, you'll bend it. These clamps don't work like C-clamps. They pivot about the spindle and the center of the flange. That pivot action can cup the surface the clamp is mounted on, perhaps up to ⅛" or more.

FIXING THE JIG

It's easy enough to make a jig do everything you want it to without providing any means for attaching it to something solid like a workbench. I've done it; it's very frustrating, so don't you do it, too. As you design a jig or fixture, include a feature to be used to hold the jig; it's always necessary (Figure 2-24).

CALIBRATION AND ADJUSTABILITY

Calibration is a means of adjusting and proving your fixture can do what it's designed to do. For example, all my tenon-making tools are adjustable; the first one, long since committed to firewood, was not. While it is possible to make a jig with no adjustability, it is risky. Things do change shape, you can't make a perfect jig, and it is possible you may drop it or run a cutter into a vital part of it. One way of accommodating such a calamity is to make the vital parts replaceable and adjustable. You may even want to make the critical components in pairs or in triplicate, just in case (Figure 2-25).

You now have some concept of just what makes a good jig. Keep these ideas in mind as you make them.

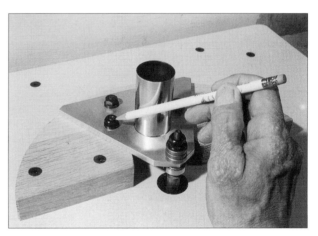

Figure 2-25
The ¼" bolts in this pin router fixture are centered in ⁹⁄₃₂" holes so I can adjust it concentric to the cutter.

Figure 2-24
The stick on the back of my mortiser has two T-nuts in it. Clamp knobs go through the bench into the nuts to secure it.

CHAPTER THREE
Right-Angle Template

A right-angle template has a fence (or hook) on its underside that automatically positions itself perpendicular (90°) to the reference edge of the work (Figures 3-1, 3-2). I use it mainly for stopped and through cuts across the grain such as for dadoes and dovetail ways and for squaring the ends of big sticks or panels. Its easy adjustment also makes it handy for on-end cuts (Figure 3-3).

A collar guide or shank-bearing guided cutter is essential for any cut with this template. Cuttings with 90° templates can be inside (dadoes) or outside (tenons). Nevertheless, the cuts are always done at the edge of the template, and they are usually single depth. Therefore, fixed-base routers are the routers of choice here (see chapter one). Edge cuts always use less than half of the router's base plate and therefore present a stability and control problem. An offset subbase should always be used to gain back that control. In fact, expect less than desirable results without one.

A 90° template and router have several advantages over table sawn and conventional router and clamp-down fence techniques. For one, the indexing process is very straight forward, and the location of the template is a direct measurement to the work's end; no scribing is necessary. The center of the bit's path is calcu-

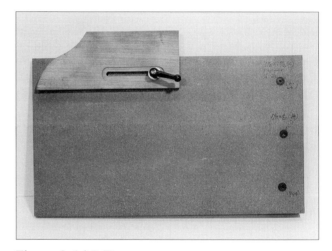

Figure 3-1A&B
This right-angle template can be used off either edge but only the right edge has an adjustable stop for stopped cuts. The hook can be adjusted precisely 90° to the edge. (Top and bottom views.)

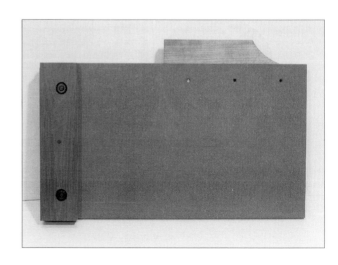

Figure 3-2
The specialized sliding template has a toggle clamp and a sliding bar of steel screw-clamped to the bench to lock it in place.

Figure 3-3
The template is just great for controlled on-end cuts such as this lap dovetail.

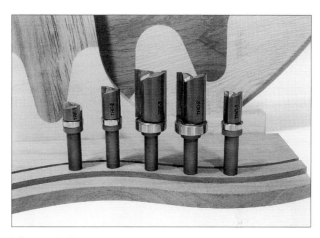

Figure 3-4
The PRC cutter set is designed for three ranges of material thicknesses to 1½". They've also designed the system for two-stage cutting; the first cutter leaves a uniform ⅟₁₆" overhang while the flush trimmer (the second stage) trims the work even with the template.

lated by adding half the collar or bearing diameter to the required distance from the end of stock. All of this is on the upside of the stock, too—unlike table saws and router tables—so you can see what's going on. Another advantage is the predictability of the cut and the ability to stay above the chip clutter and surface tear-out, both of which foul the footway of a router directly on the surface of the stock.

THE TEMPLATE

The surface of the template should be of MDF. Stock from ⅜" and up is acceptable, ½" and ⅝" being my first choices. Keep in mind for every ⅛" of template thickness, you lose ⅛" of access to the work, especially with collar guides. For shallow cuts (less than ¾") this means nothing, but for deep cuts it can be a problem. PRC (see sources) is aware of the dilemma, and they now offer a family of trimmer cutters (Model No. TR-SET) to accommodate template and work-piece variations up to 1½" (Figure 3-4).

MDF is respectable material for templates. It

is hungry for a finish however. I've used Watco Antique Oil followed with wax quite successfully. It preserves the edges, too. You should consider some sealing, but don't waste time with plastic laminate.

The width of the template should be 9" to 10", and the length should be longer than your work is wide. You might want to make left- and right-handed models and maybe two or three lengths to cover your needs.

The Fence

Make the fence out of hardwood 1"-thick by 2³⁄₁₆"-wide and a length about as wide as your template. If you use only one edge, you might want to make the fence a few inches longer for more stability. A fence of this cross section will accept toggle clamps nicely.

Adjustable Stop

There are occasions when a stopped dado or other stopped cut is necessary. The easiest way to accomplish this without radical surgery to the template is to make a separate wide rabbeted stick with a slot in it. You can then put a screw through it or a fancy studded lever to lock it. Tap the MDF in several locations to extend its

use. The stop here is a subbase stop, not a collar or bearing stop. The stop is simply adjusted to run into the subbase. The purpose of the rabbet is to aid in guiding the sliding stop along the work edge of the template. You may want to use two screws to hold the stop if you're heavy-handed.

CONSTRUCTION DETAILS

STEP 1.   Select some MDF and square it up in the usual manner. (My example is ½"x9"x16".)

STEP 2.   Square up a 1"x2³⁄₁₆"x12" piece of hardwood for the fence.

STEP 3.   Square up a ¾"x3⅜"x15" to 20" length of hardwood for the stop.

STEP 4.   Drill and tap the MDF (where necessary) as shown in the drawing (Figure 3-5). Use a ¹³⁄₆₄" high-speed steel (HSS) brad point bit for the tap (¼-20) pilot hole.

Figure 3-6
Clamp the fence down on the template while squaring it to the working edge. Lightly transfer punch the outside holes onto the fence with the ¹³⁄₆₄" punch.

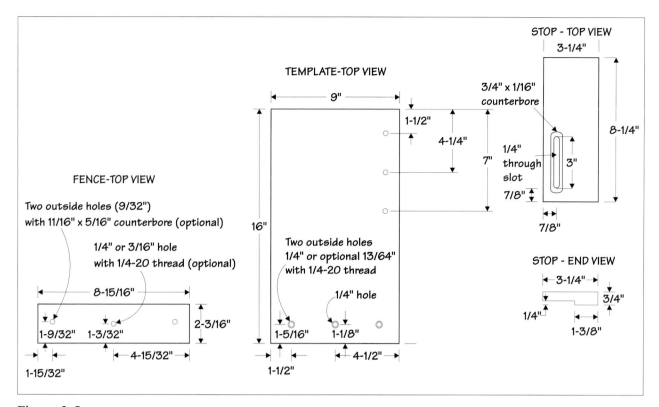

Figure 3-5
90° template.

STEP 5.   Locate and clamp the fence as shown (Figure 3-6). It has to be 90° to the work edge, but it needn't be flush to the back edge. Use a $^{13}/_{64}$" transfer punch to locate the holes for the fence.

STEP 6.   Drill the two outside holes with a $^{9}/_{32}$" HSS brad point. The center hole can be tapped for a ¼-20 thread or drilled to ¼" (see Figure 3-5). The idea here is to pivot the fence on the center hole and calibrate and square it up by means of the slop in the $^{9}/_{32}$" holes. The center hole can be tapped or drilled for the center screw; it makes little difference which. If you really want to get fancy, counterbore holes for the nuts. The nuts are spe-

cial and expensive flange nuts (available from Reid Tool Supply Co., catalog No. FNC-1). For precision work you'll need an $^{11}/_{16}$" counterbore (J&L Supply, catalog No. IPC-40044-B) and pilot (J&L Supply, catalog No. IPP-35220-B). A thin-walled ½" socket will just fit inside the counterbore.

STEP 7.   Adjust the template 90° to the fence, and then tighten the screws and/or nuts.

Making the Stop

STEP 1. Cut a ¼"x3" slot, centered 1" from either edge (Figure 3-5). Note the extraordinary length for this piece (15" to 20") is for your safety. Tunneling, slotting, etc. can't be done safely on a short workpiece.

STEP 2. Counterbore a ¹⁄₁₆"-deep by ¾"-wide seat for a ¾" washer if desired. Use a plunge router with an edge guide for both cuts. If you change to a ¾" cutting diameter bit after slotting, leaving all the stops fixed, the counterbore will be automatically centered.

STEP 3. Now excavate a ¼"-deep by 1⅛"-wide long-grain tunnel on the slotted side of the work. Do this on the router table leaving ⅛" of uncut material for support. Then saw away the ⅛" support after the tunnel is complete (Figure 3-7) and cut to length.

STEP 4. Snug up the rabbet shoulder to the working edge of the template and mark several locations through the slot for your holdfast. Tap ¼-20 holes if desired and use a fancy adjustable lock lever (Reid Tool Supply Co., Cat. No. KHB-58) as a clamp/knob. A common nut and bolt will also work.

A STOPPED DADO

The cheapest, sweetest way to make a stopped dado is with a 1" (use Porter-Cable 42030) collar guide and the appropriate bit.

STEP 1. Position the template as desired, adding ½" to the measurement to account for the collar offset. Let's

Figure 3-7
The underside of the stop. Leaving ⅛" of uncut material allows you to slot a wide swath without tipping the stock accidentally. Sawing off the ⅛"x¼" support creates the rabbet.

Figure 3-8
Since the stop is trapped on the template, you can adjust it with one hand. A second screw may be necessary to firmly fix the stop for all-day use.

say you want a dado 10" from the end of your board. Set the template 10½" from the end for the center of your cutter to fall on 10".

STEP 2. Lower the cutter to just brush the surface of the stock. Now slide the

Figure 3-9
I'm pulling and pushing the router to the left so the collar guide never deviates from the template. If I follow the heavy black line on the template (knob over line), the same section of the template guide is always in contact with the edge of the template. This practice cancels out the effect of any cutter/-collar eccentricities.

tool so the tool bit is tangent to your stop/scribe line. Slide and lock your subbase stop against the subbase (Figure 3-8).

STEP 3. Set the depth of cut and rout, never letting the collar guide stray from the edge of the template (Figure 3-9).

Note: For cuts ¾" wide and less than ⁵⁄₁₆" deep, a 1½ hp tool is adequate. If the crosscut is a dovetail slot, always consider preplowing the cut with a straight bit. All day work cutting deep wide dadoes should be done in two passes with a 2 hp tool or greater.

CHAPTER FOUR
The Notching Jig

Figure 4-1
The more stuff that articulates well with the members of a joint, the stronger the joint. This notched corner brace is an example.

Square corner notches don't have a lot of application, but if and when you need one, it would be nice to be able to make one well without a lot of jigging, risk or forethought. With my jig you will find the process easy and safe, but you won't spend much time making it, and you'll get perfect results. Moreover, I've built a few other functions into the jig for specialty

joinery if you ever get into that closet.

Notches are handy in shelving and panels where you might want them to nest around a square leg. Often inside corner braces require a notch for the same reason (Figure 4-1). I use a stick with a corner notch in it to guide my square corner chisel (Figure 4-2). Dust panel frames, drawer accessories and, yes, even jigs

Figure 4-2

These square corner chisels are really handy in dressing up mortises. Positioning and clamping the notched guide at the corners guarantees a good result every time you smack the chisel.

Figure 4-3

I need a little more travel from this stop. I routed the notch in it to clear the clamp flange.

and fixtures on occasion need corner notches (Figure 4-3). My jig is also a template for excavating a dovetail patch (Figure 4-4). It can also produce a dovetail way to lock a half lap (Figure 4-5), aid in cutting minor excavations for shelf hangers and pins on the ends of shelves, and guide the cutter for the shoulders of a lap dovetail. I'll show you the setups for those cuts latter on, but first let's get some background on the notch itself.

Square corner notching is one of those operations that can be done on a lot of tools, but, in my view, it is best done with a router (Figure 4-6). You can do it on the radial, table or band saw but at some risk. On a table saw, the work has to be held on edge and on end, and it must be well fixtured to be done safely. Moreover, stops need to be set, and usually more than one blade height setting is required. It can be done on the band saw with the work flat, but there are always saw blade chatter marks to contend with. The radial saw has its approach problems, and, in the hands of the hand craftsman, the

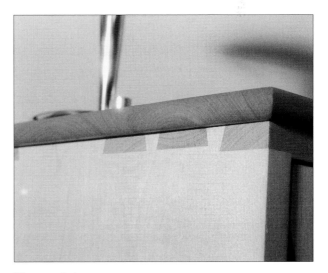

Figure 4-4

These dovetails are really patches glued into sockets after assembly. The cabinet was assembled with just a shallow tongue and groove.

Figure 4-5

The finished reinforced joint. Note that I dovetailed the half lap itself. The lap assembly is a lot easier if you can jam one of the pieces into a dovetail shoulder like this.

backsaw is slow and requires a lot of skill to do well. The router has its limitations, too, but they're relatively modest in comparison.

Due to the design and lengths of straight bits and to safety considerations, I've restricted the jig to cut notches less than 2"x2". Most plunge routers used on the jig will span the template opening without dipping into it if its base diameter is 6" or more. If you need a wider notch, you can make the window wider, but you'll need an auxiliary subbase wider than twice the window width you select. The cutter depth maximums, however, should remain at 2". You're advised to make your first jig like mine, get a feel for the process and then improve on it to suit your needs. In my view, jumping into uncharted waters should be done without weights on.

MAKING THE JIG

There are four pieces to this tool, and none of them is critical. There's a vertical work-holding panel surface, the horizontal router platform,

the stop and the jig holding arm. A ⅜"-thick template with a 3⅛"-wide by 4"-deep notch cut into it is also needed as a guide to rout the openings in the two panels. A drill press should be used to do all the drilling. To rout with the template, a 1½ hp router and ¾"- to 1"-long flush trimming bit (Whiteside Machine Co. 3015 or equivalent) should be used.

Figure 4-6

This notch was cut with the straight bit in the background. It only takes a second.

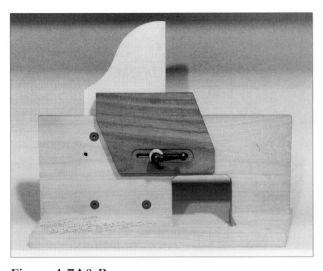 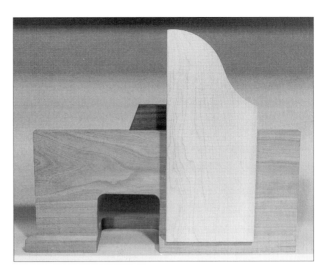

Figure 4-7A&B

I made the jig from an old piece of cherry, a scrap of rosewood and a maple cutoff. Front (above) and back (above right) views.

Setting Out

STEP 1. Make the template as shown (see Figure 4-8C), and be sure to keep all the cuttings 90° to each other and parallel.

STEP 2. The vertical panel (Figure 4-8D) is a ¾"x5¼"x13¼" rectangle. Position the template 3¹⁄₁₆" from one end and rout a 2¼"x3⅛" notch out of it. Waste most of the excavation with the band saw before routing.

STEP 3. Drill the four ¼" holes and counter-sink for the jig holding arm. (Note: I'm using ¼-20 machine screws to fasten the jig holding arm, but #10 or #12 sheet metal screws will also work.)

STEP 4. The horizontal panel (Figure 4-8B) starts as a ⅝"x5⅜"x13½" panel. Cut a 4"x3⅛" notch in it as shown.

STEP 5. Next, on the router table, cut a ³⁄₁₆"-deep by ¾"-wide slot centered 1⅛" from the front edge.

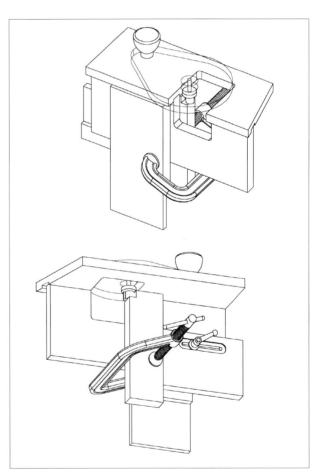

Figure 4-8A

View over and under work surface (horizontal panel) of cutting in action.

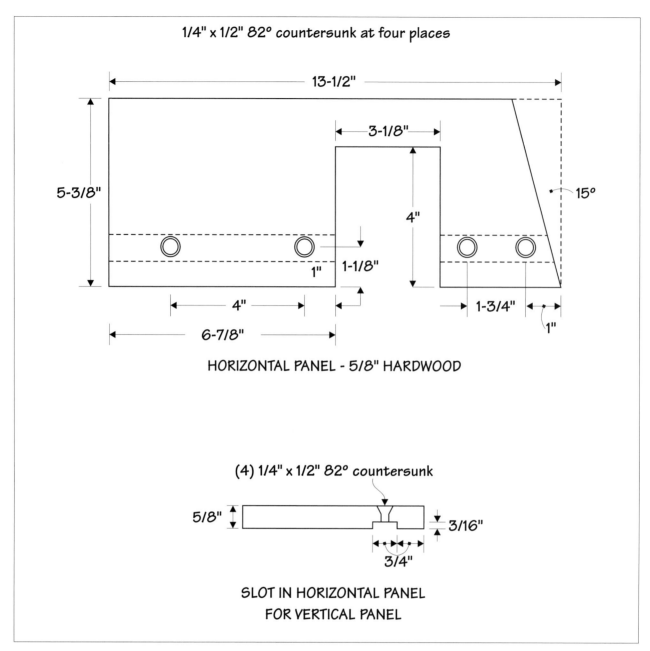

HORIZONTAL PANEL - 5/8" HARDWOOD

SLOT IN HORIZONTAL PANEL
FOR VERTICAL PANEL

Figure 4-8B

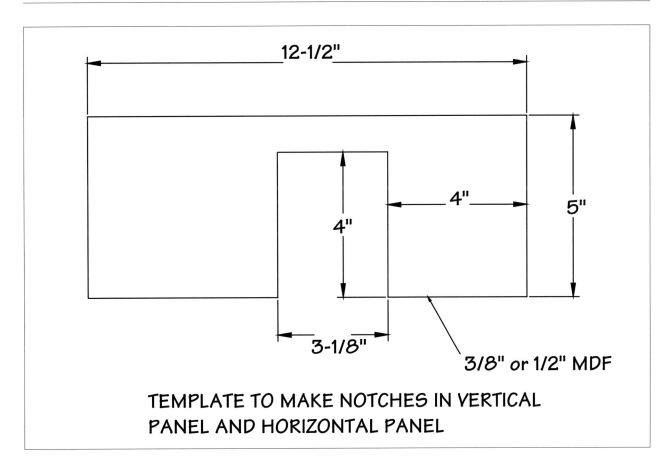

TEMPLATE TO MAKE NOTCHES IN VERTICAL PANEL AND HORIZONTAL PANEL

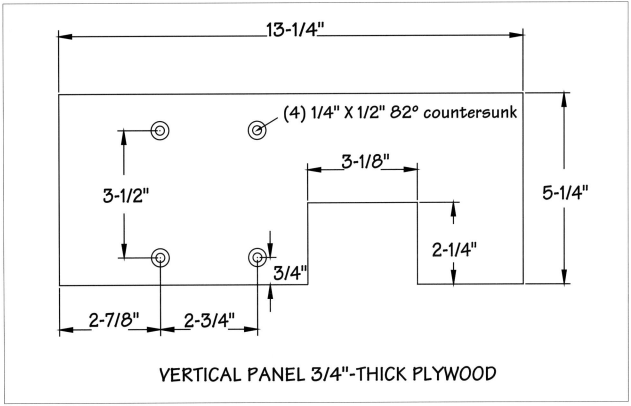

VERTICAL PANEL 3/4"-THICK PLYWOOD

Figure 4-8C&D

Figure 4-9

Mark the vertical panel every 2" or so through the slot with a ¼" transfer punch.

Figure 4-10

Keep the jig holding arm about ⁵⁄₁₆" away from the window. If it was placed in the window, it would be whittled away with use.

STEP 6. Saw an approximate 80° included angle on the end nearest the notch.

STEP 7. Now drill the four ¼"-diameter holes and countersink for flathead 1¼" x ¼-20 machine screws (Figure 4-8D).

STEP 8. Align the notches of the two panels and transfer the hole pattern onto the edge grain of the vertical panel. Drill and tap for the screws in step 7.

Making the Stop

The stop is similar to the one used in the previous chapter except the rabbet is much wider. The zigzag cuttings are decorative; a rectangle will work just as well.

STEP 1. As before, rip a 15"- to 20"-long piece of hardwood into a 4" width. Rout a ¼"-wide through slot 2⅜" long centered 1" from an edge. Then rout a ¹⁄₁₆"-deep by ¾"-wide counterbore for a ¾"-diameter washer (the drawing in Figure 4-8F shows it in stages).

STEP 2. Cut a wide full-length tunnel on the slotted side of the stock. Leave the first ⅛" of the stock full thickness for support. You'll rip it off later, so the slot will be centered ⅞" from the edge. The tunnel should be about 2⅞"-wide. Its length is not critical, but make it at least 2⅞"-wide by 6"-long.

STEP 3. Position the stop with its rabbet against the bottom of the jig and make a transfer mark through the slot onto the vertical panel (Figure 4-9). Just exactly where to drill along this line is arbitrary. If you drill and tap every 2½" across the full length of the panel, then the stop should stop wherever you want it to.

STEP 4. Drill and tap for the ¼-20 thread of the clamp-lock lever.

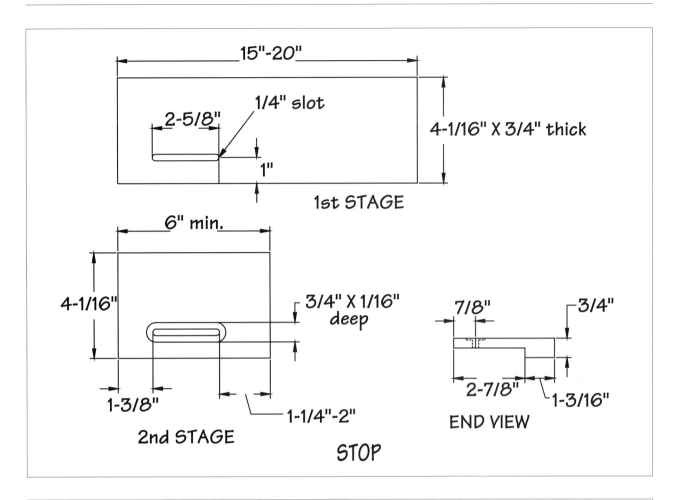

15"-20"

1/4" slot

2-5/8"

4-1/16" X 3/4" thick

1"

1st STAGE

6" min.

4-1/16"

3/4" X 1/16" deep

1-3/8"

1-1/4"-2"

2nd STAGE

STOP

7/8"

3/4"

2-7/8"

1-3/16"

END VIEW

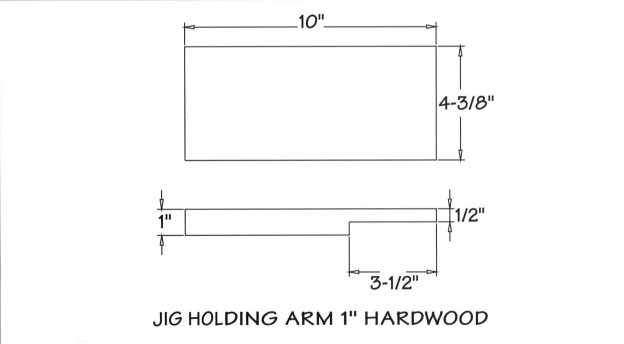

10"

4-3/8"

1"

1/2"

3-1/2"

JIG HOLDING ARM 1" HARDWOOD

Figure 4-8E&F

Figure 4-11
You may want to use a spring clamp to hold the work as you adjust the stop.

Figure 4-12
This is the setup you want to avoid. Although I can successfully notch from this side (left) of the window, any cutter deviation from the template will spoil the cut.

THE JIG HOLDING ARM

The ability of a jig to be positioned and held fast is as important as the function of the jig itself; don't abbreviate it. The best material for this component is wood. I've taken the liberty to stylize it, but it's strictly a folly of mine. It has no function, and the cyma cutout is omitted in the drawing.

STEP 1. Size a piece of hardwood to 1"x4⅜" x10".
STEP 2. Waste a ½"-deep by 3½"-wide lap into one end.
STEP 3. Assemble the two panels, and position the jig holding arm ⁵⁄₁₆" away from the window on the outside of the jig opposite the stop and butted up against the underside of the horizontal router platform (Figure 4-10).
STEP 4. Now transfer the screw hole pattern from the vertical panel onto the arm. Drill four ¹³⁄₆₄" holes ⅞" deep and tap for four 1¼"-long ¼-20 flathead machine screws; you're ready to rout.

NOTCHING

Notching can be accomplished with straight bits and collars or with shank-bearing guided straight cutters. Deep, wide excavations should be done with a plunge router and collar guide at multidepth settings. Cuttings less than 1"-square can be done with a fixed-base router and bearing-guided cutter at full depth. Remember, when using bearing-guided cutters, the cutter might accidentally slice into the opening, thus spoiling the edge. A collar guide will prevent this from happening.

STEP 1. Turn the jig upside down and rest the end of the work against the underside of horizontal panel.
STEP 2. Adjust its position into the window opening, and slide and lock the fence against the edge of the stock. Clamp securely with one or more C-clamps (Figure 4-11).

Figure 4-13
This small box has withstood more than twelve years of seasonal dimensional stress with only one lap dovetail.

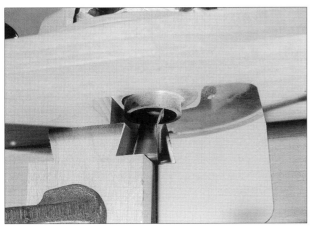

Figure 4-14
The second half of this dovetail is as easy to cut as the first. Clamp securely; unnecessary vibration is your enemy.

STEP 3. Upend the jig, and clamp the jig holding arm in a vise. Pull and push the work and the jig to make sure it won't move.

STEP 4. Choose your router, cutter and/or collar. Adjust the depth, and carve away the notch (Figure 4-6).

Note: Although it is possible to rout from either or both edges of the window with the stock fully into the window, don't do it. The cutter will be trapped and can run away from you in the event of an accident (Figure 4-12). If the cutter and collar wander away from the edge of the window, the cutter will plow its own random pathway. Position only that portion of stock into the window you'd like to waste away.

LAP DOVETAIL TENON

Lap dovetails are often used to hold cabinets and desk sides together. Small boxes can also be held together with lap dovetails (Figure 4-13). The procedure for making the cuts is essentially the same as for cutting notches.

STEP 1. Position the stock into the window as before and adjust and lock the fence.

STEP 2. Use a collar guide and the appropriate dovetail cutter, set to depth and rout to the window edge.

STEP 3. For centered dovetails, reverse the work and cut the second shoulder (Figure 4-14).

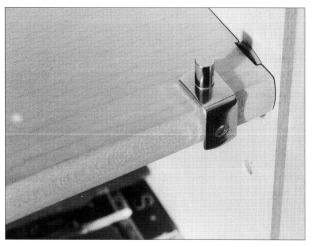

Figure 4-15
The notch reveals just a little bit of the hanger. A thicker shelf would hide it altogether.

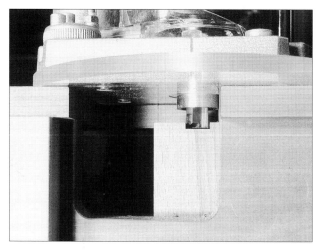

Figure 4-16
This is a single-pass inside cut. Any deviation from the template will spoil the cut. Fortunately, there is no stress on the cutter with such a shallow cut.

SHELF NOTCHING FOR PINNED HARDWARE

For a nicer fit when hanging shelves with right-angle shelf pins, excavate a ¹⁄₁₆"-deep by ⁹⁄₁₆"-wide notch (four places) into the ends of your shelving (Figure 4-15).

STEP 1.   Position the shelf on end and set the stop (fence).

STEP 2.   Use an Amana 45428 or equivalent set to ¹⁄₁₆" to make the cut (Figure 4-16). Any collar whose inside diameter is greater than ⅝" (Porter-Cable 42039) will guide the tool nicely across end of the the shelf.

SHELF NOTCH FOR ¼" STEEL DOWELS

The next grade up for shelf hanging, in my view, uses ¼" steel dowel pins stuck into the sides of the cabinet. The shelves can be cut to full length, and, since the shelf houses the pins,

they're essentially invisible. The system is beautiful, but your holes have to be drilled accurately, and your indexing in the jig must be consistent. If possible, use the same edge as the reference for all four cuttings.

STEP 1.   Locate and clamp the shelf. Adjust the stop and upend the jig as before.

STEP 2.   Select a collar and ¼" diameter cutter, preferably solid carbide, such as an Amana 45111-SC.

STEP 3.   Set the depth of cut equal to the length of the pins poking out of the cabinet plus ¹⁄₁₆" or so, typically ¾". A plunge router might be better here, cutting in two or three passes (Figures 4-17A, B, C, D).

DOVETAIL SOCKETS FOR CABINET PLATE JOINERY

Hand- or machine-cut dovetail joinery for cabinets is a highly disciplined technique. Not only must you be good at material preparation, layout, sawing (and/or routing) and chiseling, but you've got to be a good assembler with lots of patience.

If you could put a box together with, say, a lousy tongue and groove or even dowels, you can, after assembly, dovetail it! (See Figure 4-4.) With the jig holding arm and sliding stop

Figure 4-17A
Keep the collar against the window, lest you'll spoil the cut. The cutter should cut about one diameter (¼") into the stock.

Figure 4-17B
I've cut the notch and the pin radius without moving the stock, so they coincide.

Figure 4-17C
Hardware in place.

Figure 4-17D
Hardware in place. (Another view, inverted.)

Figure 4-18

This 8° dovetail cutter (Jesada 818-706) is the largest of all production-made dovetail bits. This excavation is ¾" deep; you've got to preplow the area with a straight bit first.

Figure 4-19

I've set the outfeed side of my router fence to take just a .005" pass. Since this is a full-thickness cut, it is wise to take just a little at a time.

removed, you can clamp my notcher to your cabinet, excavate a dovetail socket and make a dovetail patch (plate) to bridge the cabinet sides and top (and bottom). A good serviceable joint is possible, and not a lot of skill is required.

STEP 1.   Build your cabinet and glue it together.

STEP 2.   Clamp the notcher (now used as a horizontal half-blind notcher) to your cabinet, and rout a dovetail socket at centers and depths of your choosing (Figure 4-18).

Note: Use different collar diameters to control the width of the socket and different depths of cut to vary the pattern. You may want to preplow with another router with the same, or larger, diameter collar if your dovetail cutter is laboring.

STEP 3.   Make the plate with a jointer where the fence is set to the angle of the dovetail bit. Shave a little at a time until the patch slip fits into the socket. A router table with an adjustable outfeed fence and dovetail bit is a good alternative (Figure 4-19).

Note: The thickness of the material for the plate should not be more than .005" thicker than the socket is deep. To get a perfect fit at the back corners will take some careful routing, as the corners are radiused and dovetailed; you may also chisel the corners square as I did (Figures 4-20, 4-21).

Figure 4-20
Close up of squared corner.

Figure 4-21
Glued-up and dressed.

THROUGH DOVETAIL PINS TO LOCK THE HALF LAP

You may have wondered what the 20° angle on the end of the horizontal panel is for. Well, on occasion, you may want to lock or decorate a half lap. Half laps are fairly strong but they rely heavily on glue to function. If you can carefully cut a dovetail pathway or two across a lap, you can insert keyways that lock up the joint. This is not merely symbolic; it really works.

STEP 1. Create and glue your lap together in the usual way.

Figure 4-22
This template has a lot of clamping face. Squareness is not critical; in fact, the cutter pathway off this template is 20° from perpendicular to offer more dovetail pin engagement. The work is sandwiched between two pieces of scrap to prevent any tear out.

Figure 4-23
I cut two small dovetail ways here using a Jesada 818-097 cutter. Note how clean the entry and exit ways are.

Figure 4-25
I don't usually get too sloppy with glue, but dovetails do jam, and a lot of glue allows for an easier fit in this case. No clamping is necessary.

STEP 2. Create a sandwich of scrap-work-scrap and clamp it in the fixture (without the sliding stop). Position the lap, perhaps centered, at the angled end of the jig (Figure 4-22).

STEP 3. Rout, with collar and dovetail bit, right through the package, keeping the collar against the template at all times (Figure 4-23). If the dovetail bit is struggling, preplow with a straight bit.

STEP 4. Rout a long-grain dovetail key on the router table; insert it in the keyway. Saw away the waste and sand flush (Figures 4-23, 4-24, 4-25, 4-5). The jig is a bit goofy and esoteric, but so is woodworking. Jigs and fixtures, an art unto themselves, are the keys to smart and useful ordinary cutting chores.

Figure 4-24
Rout a centered pin on stock wide enough to hold safely on edge. Let the fit be snug, but no hammer fits, knocking or rocking.

CHAPTER FIVE
The Clamping Template

Efficient and safe routing requires clamping and crowding (blocking in) the stock. Templates simplify cutting and in the same breath provide lots of surface for easy routing. This symbiosis of surface and hardware provides for the safest of cutting procedures. This jig is handy for both hand and table routers, and you may also want to use it on the table saw.

I derived this jig after several close calls routing short and narrow stock. Hand routing small workpieces is particularly difficult because the clamps are always in the way, and when untoggled templates are used, the work squirms and the templates shift. With the use of this jig, this never happens; moreover, you can index the work, load and unload the work quickly, and rout nearly with reckless abandonment.

I use the fixture to safely make very wide rabbets on the router table, joint narrow short stock, round over square stock for dowels, taper legs and do other miscellaneous cuttings. There isn't much to the jig: some toggle clamps, MDF and a fence will do it. Let's make the thing and then demonstrate some cuts.

JIG DESCRIPTION
The jig is made for work about 6"x24" or smaller. If you plan to use it for longer or very

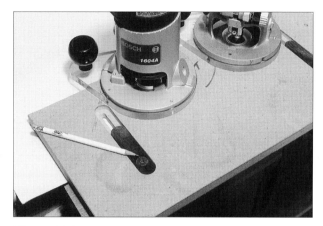

Figure 5-1
This is the operator side of the jig (while hand routing). These flathead cap screws are located right on the center of the clamp flanges. The rosewood washers spread the force of the screw over a large area.

short stock, you should size the template accordingly. The template, as designed, will hold work as narrow as ⅜"-thick by ⅝"-wide. Certainly if you are doing a run of samples that are all the same size, you should make the jig fit your work exactly.

I've chosen ¾" MDF for the basic substrate, and although that may seem thick, you will find that it's just right for the jobs I use it for. Furthermore, thinner stock may flex under heavy clamp loads and spoil the accuracy of

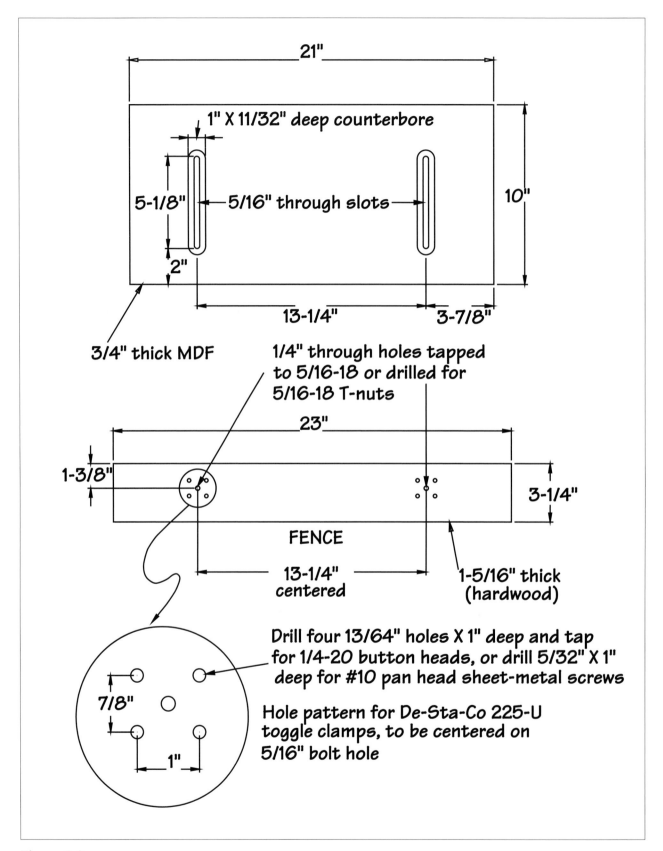

21"

1" X 11/32" deep counterbore

5-1/8" — 5/16" through slots

10"

2"

13-1/4" 3-7/8"

3/4" thick MDF

1/4" through holes tapped to 5/16-18 or drilled for 5/16-18 T-nuts

23"

1-3/8"

FENCE

3-1/4"

13-1/4" centered

1-5/16" thick (hardwood)

Drill four 13/64" holes X 1" deep and tap for 1/4-20 button heads, or drill 5/32" X 1" deep for #10 pan head sheet-metal screws

Hole pattern for De-Sta-Co 225-U toggle clamps, to be centered on 5/16" bolt hole

7/8"

1"

Figure 5-2

Template and fence.

your cuts and the jig. One reason the jig stays as flat as it does is that the fasteners are located right in the center of clamp flanges, and the stresses are distributed evenly with a pair of $\frac{5}{16}$"x4" rosewood washers on the operator side of the jig. These washers are recessed into the fiberboard so the pathway for the hand router is completely clear of clutter and clamps (Figure 5-1).

MAKING THE JIG

STEP 1.   Begin by preparing a $\frac{3}{4}$"x10"x21" piece of MDF. The edges should be defect free since any one of them can be used for a collar- or bearing-guided cut.

STEP 2.   Cut two $\frac{5}{16}$"-wide through slots, as shown in the drawing (Figure 5-2). Then counterbore the slots to about $\frac{5}{16}$"-deep by 1"-wide. Use a $\frac{5}{16}$"-diameter straight bit for the slot and a 1" straight bit for the counterbore. One easy way of doing this is with a template with a slot $1\frac{35}{64}$" wide cut into it. The slot should allow about $5\frac{3}{4}$" of travel for a Porter-Cable 42048 collar (diameter $1\frac{35}{64}$"). To produce such a template, space a pair of $\frac{3}{8}$" fiberboard straightedges $1\frac{35}{64}$" apart, screw them down onto another $\frac{3}{8}$" piece of MDF template, and rout out the space (Figure 5-3). While routing the slot and counterbore in the work, pay attention not to move the template. Use the same collar (Porter-Cable 42048) for both cuts. This automatically centers the counterbore to the slot. You must rout the counterbore first; doing it after the slot will result in a torn slot.

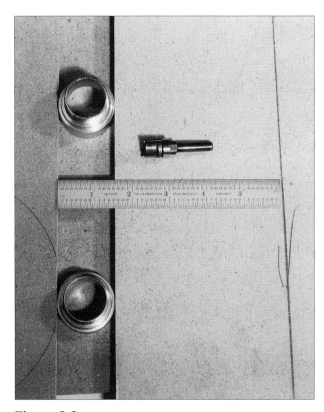

Figure 5-3
Two Porter-Cable template collars, catalog no. 42048, establish the correct spacing for the templates to make the template! After mapping out the area (about $6\frac{1}{4}$"x$1\frac{35}{64}$"), jigsaw out the waste, and rout flush with a PRC TA-170 or equivalent flush trimming bit.

STEP 3.   Cut a piece of straight-grained hardwood (I used walnut) to $1\frac{5}{16}$"x$3\frac{1}{4}$"x 23". Lay out the hole pattern in it as shown in the drawing. The centers for the $\frac{5}{16}$" screws can be found by using a transfer punch in the slots of the template. A T-nut can be used for receiving the $\frac{5}{16}$" hold-down bolt, or you may wish to tap the wood as I did. In my opinion, one of the best clamps for this jig is the De-Sta-Co 225-U. Its flange-hole pattern, front to back, is 1" and from side to side is

Figure 5-4

The 1"-square blank is hanging over the edge of the template by ⁹⁄₁₆". Any less, the cutter may nip the template. Once you've routed with the field completely clear of any obstacles, you may decide to do any template cut this way; it's so safe.

Figure 5-5

I've left some material uncut so the clamp can get hold of it, and it won't rotate. Large roundovers require a lot of power and engage a lot of work; you've got to keep a good grip on them. Stops on either end will keep the work from turning into an "arrow." (Shown upside down.)

⅞". If you use another clamp, drill accordingly. Number 10x¾" pan head sheet-metal screws are acceptable, so drill for them as desired. For me, ¼-20x¾" buttonheads are my first choice. Threading the stock is, of course, required for any machine screw.

STEP 4. The 1"x4" washers are cut from ¹¹⁄₃₂" rosewood (aluminum or steel is also acceptable). You can round the ends to match the end of the counterbore or square the end corners of the counterbore to match a square-ended washer. The washers swim (slide) 2" in the slots, hence the fence travels about 2". The fence can also pivot so tapers are possible without any modifications. Due to the offset center lines of the fence slots, you can work stock from ¾" to about 6" wide by reversing the fence and working off the opposite edge.

MAKING ROUNDS FROM SQUARES

You can rout squares round by quarter-rounding each corner of a square. Dowels (or rounds) can be made of any species to match or contrast with the project you're working on. I've made dowels from ¾" to 1½" in diameter. Smaller rounds are too hard to hold safely, and bigger ones (larger than 1½") require cutters too big for a hand router. Cuttings can safely be made on the router table with large router bits.

Procedure

STEP 1. Mill some stock to square dimensions. Pay particular attention to squareness as any deviation here will yield an out-of-round later. Oversize the stock by about .005" in both dimensions to allow for some sanding to clean up the mill marks.

Figure 5-6

Stops are set for the start and end of the cut to preserve some square section for holding. I rarely do stopped cuttings on the router table, but I'm not afraid this time; I've got the whole template assembly between me and the cutter.

STEP 2.　Set the fence of the jig to project more than one radius of material beyond the edge of the template: ¹⁄₁₆" to ⅛" maximum (Figure 5-4). Set the clamp spindles for thickness of stock.

STEP 3.　(Hand router.) Select the roundover and adjust the depth of cut for slightly less than one radius. Many roundover bits are odd sized in spite of specs to the contrary. Plan on a little bit of sanding, and rout .003" to .006" (a paper thickness) less than one radius.

STEP 4.　Rout one quarter, rotate the work 90° counterclockwise (as viewed from the left end on end), rout a corner and so on (Figure 5-5).

Router Table

STEP 1.　Set up the work in the template as before.

Figure 5-7

It's quite possible to hold ⁺⁄₋.003" on the diameter of the dowel if you mill squarely and your sanding caul is accurate. The finished dowel measures close to its 1" target.

STEP 2.　Consider using an ovolo instead of the roundover. A bearing is unnecessary in the router table. Use a Jesada 827-627, ½" radius or equivalent. A half-round tool bit is also acceptable.

STEP 3.　Set the cutter as before, just under 1" radius, and rout each corner using the fence as the guide. In order to keep the work from turning on the last quarter, and for easier clamping, keep the first and last 1" unmilled (Figure 5-6).

STEP 4.　Sand the dowel with a concave sanding caul, perhaps one produced by the corresponding core box cutter—one with the same radius as the roundover (Figure 5-7).

Figure 5-8

This work will see a full ½"x1³⁄₁₆" of cutter. The material is 1¼" beyond the edge. Incorporate a stop for easy load and to prevent a "fly-back."

Figure 5-9

My fence can pivot about 1" before I have to relocate the whole fence assembly.

Wide Rabbets

There are occasions when wide rabbets are required on narrow stock, and there is no safe way to hold the work. On this jig I've made perfect rabbets wider than 2½"! The stops in the earlier chapters can be made safely on this tool.

STEP 1.   Project more material beyond the edge of the template than you plan to rout (¹⁄₁₆" to ⅛"), adjust the fence, and use stops if desired for easy reload (Figure 5-8).

STEP 2.   Project the cutter to its maximum north/south position, and provide a means to reposition the fence for cuts wider than the cutter diameter (Figure 5-9).

STEP 3.   Proceed routing, keeping the east/west depth of cut to less than ³⁄₁₆" per pass for cuts greater than ½" north/south. Wider cuts are permissible for cuttings less than ½".

Jointing

A jointer is the best tool to square edges and flatten faces, but it does have its limitations. Very big or very small sticks are hard to joint. This jig, with a bearing- or collar-guided tool, can joint stuff down to ¾" in width or less.

STEP 1.   Project just enough material beyond the template edge to true the stick.

STEP 2.   Select a bearing-guided cutter with a flute length nicely matched to the thickness of stock and rout against the template left to right (Figure 5-10).

Figure 5-10

For medium-thickness cutting, this Whiteside ⅜" shanked x ⅞" O. D. (catalog no. 3045) is perfect. For the safest cut, feed left to right.

Tapering

Tapering is usually a table saw affair, but I'm not too crazy about the saw for any operation. I like this jig a lot more. There's just something about the saw—maybe it's the chips in my face, the noise; maybe it's the 60 teeth on the blade gnarling at me; or just maybe it's the chatter marks left on the work that I have to sand out that I don't like.

STEP 1. To use the jig for tapering, twist the fence to the desired angle, and clamp a stop on the template to index the work (Figure 5-11).

STEP 2. Mark the work, and band saw off most of the waste.

STEP 3. Rout away just as though you were jointing, matching the flute length to the thickness of stock. The band saw step can be simplified if the work is fed to the blade on the jig (Figure 5-12).

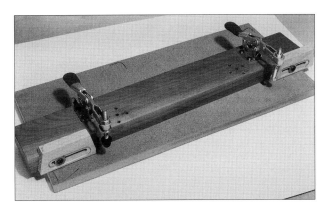

Figure 5-11

I've made a sliding stop for my jig. Clamping a stick down is permissible too. I also drilled another set of toggle clamp holes for more reach and clearance.

Figure 5-12

I've clamped a ⅜"-thick piece of MDF down on the band saw, parallel to the saw fence. There's a notch in it for the blade. Using the template as guide, now I can easily saw the work on the jig leaving a ¹⁄₁₆" overhang. This is what jigs are all about: efficiency and safety.

CHAPTER SIX
Edge Guides

Edge guides predate bearing-guided cutters by decades. They were the principle means of guiding routers parallel to the edges of stock or templates. They were used in an era when tricky hand skills were commonplace and commercial router jigging rare. Edge guides are quite common today but are not a major player when it comes to ordinary routing.

Their two principle handicaps are related to the unwieldiness of the router/edge guide package. Cuts along the edge of stock are rather forgiving as the cutter is free to pare away the edge as the operator sees fit. The cutter is not trapped in any way. Nevertheless, the start and end of the cut can be challenging because less than one-fourth of the router is on the work at either end, and the guide easily pivots around the corner at its center line which is coincident with the ends of the cut. The result? The extremes of the cut are usually boogered. The process of edge guiding can be improved substantially with an offset subbase, but a modicum of skill and practice are still necessary to achieve good results (Figure 6-1).

On inside cuts, there is no forgiveness for a momentary loss of edge contact, the second handicap. Any deviation of the guide from the edge will spoil the cut. There are a lot of competing things going on while cutting inside, whether down or cross-grain. The operator not only has the three push-down/pull-in/slide-along responsibilities, he has to contend with the dynamics of the cutter exerting its forces back into the router. If the force was zero, the cut would be about as easy as an edge cut, but it ain't. The cutter will confound your hand-feed, so hold on and experiment. If I practice for about fifteen minutes on scrap, I can usually get it right on the project stock. On the plus side, the edge guide can do a lot of the same things that a router table can with its adjustable fence. It's no substitute, mind you, but it is possible to duplicate many of its cuts. For example, with a long offset fence you can joint, you can and should use bearingless cutters with the edge guide, and both cross- and down-grain inside and outside cuts are possible. Moreover, the guide, like the fence on the router table, is infinitely adjustable and capable therefore of any width cut. In spite of this range of work, however, edge guides are used mostly for mortising in tandem with plunge routers (Figure 6-2).

Another benefit of an edge guide is its respect for the router. The edge guide tempers the lateral (sideways) stress on the cutter and armature bearings. With a bearing-guided cutter, the bearing will transmit the side forces directly into the cutter and armature, often embossing the work or invoking a little resonance (hammering) into

Figure 6-1
This ensemble of off-set subbase opposite the edge guide gives you the best control for an otherwise awkward procedure like this rabbet cut. A grip and a pull on the offset subbase knob combines the push-down and pull-in functions to that hand while the slide-along function is carried out with the other hand on the base casting.

Figure 6-2
This pair of simplified edge guides traps the router on the jig. The jig takes a while to make, as do the edge guides, but once engaged in work, the mortise can be excavated in seconds and with very little skill; the essence of jig-making.

the cut. The edge guide absorbs any excess side loads you might impose on the cutter, and since the guide edge is "averaged" over all or any edge defects, the cuts are usually cleaner than those produced from bearing-guided tools.

MAKING THE GUIDE

The edge guide you'll make is designed for the Porter-Cable 690, 100, 630 or 6931 plunge casting and my offset subbase (Porter-Cable catalog no. 42193). The auxiliary fence will allow you to use the guide with the supplied black Bakelite base (catalog no. 42186). The guide body

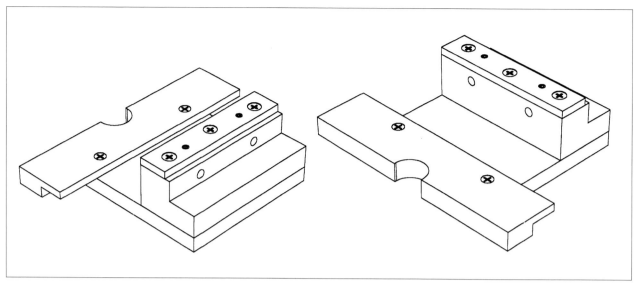

Figure 6-3E
Edge guide body for the Porter-Cable 690.

Figure 6-4
The author's 690 edge guide ready for work. The auxiliary fence is stylized as is the rod-holding block. If you can make something a little more pleasing to the eye, where's the harm?

should work for most routers, but the rods and the spacing of the rods are unique for most tools, so you'll need to account for that as necessary. Consider doing the woodwork with stock two to three times longer than the drawing dictates (Figures 6-3, 6-4). This will give you enough stock for two units or one good one if you spoil one on the setups.

Making the Edge Guide
The components of the jig are:
1. ½"x5" square maple platform.
2. Rabbeted rod-holding block 1⁷⁄₁₆"x2³⁄₁₆"x5" hardwood (walnut in my case).
3. ¼"x1"x5" setscrew aluminum holding plate.
4. Hardwood auxiliary fence ⅝"x1⅞"x8".
5. ⁹⁄₃₂"x9½" stainless rods.

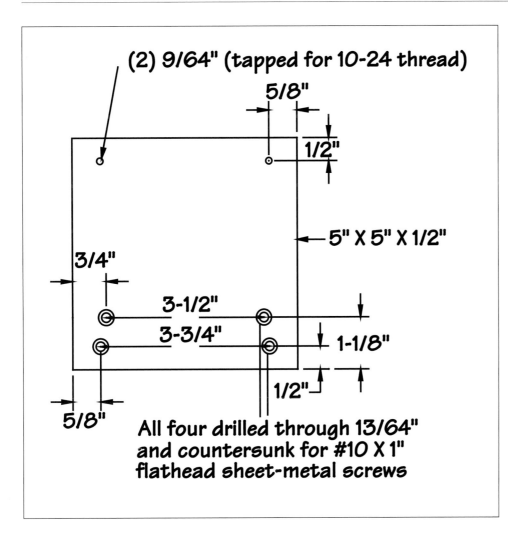

(2) 9/64" (tapped for 10-24 thread)

5/8"

1/2"

5" X 5" X 1/2"

3/4"

3-1/2"

3-3/4"

1-1/8"

1/2"

5/8"

All four drilled through 13/64" and countersunk for #10 X 1" flathead sheet-metal screws

Figure 6-3A
Square maple platform.

The Platform

STEP 1.   Make the platform out of straight, seasoned hardwood; maple or beech are both good choices. Make two or three 5" squares at ½" thickness.

STEP 2.   Drill four through holes and countersink for #10 flathead sheet-metal screws as shown. Also drill and tap two holes for two 10-24x¾" socket head flatheads (Figure 6-3A).

Rod-Holding Block

STEP 1.   Mill a prime piece of hardwood (I used slow-growth walnut) to 1⁷⁄₁₆"x2³⁄₁₆"x16" to 20" long.

STEP 2.   Grip the billet in the clamping template (chapter five), and waste away an ¹¹⁄₁₆"-deep by 1"-wide rabbet on the 2³⁄₁₆" surface (Figures 6-3B, 6-5).

STEP 3.   Cut to 5", clamp the rod-holding block flush to the rear of the platform. Transfer punch the sheet-metal hole pattern to the rod-holding block, and drill for the #10 fasteners.

STEP 4.   Drill two 7.25mm holes on 2⅜" centers as indicated in the drawing. Drill accordingly for other router castings, allowing about .002" to .004" of slop for the guide rods. (See W.L. Fuller, in Sources, for drills.)

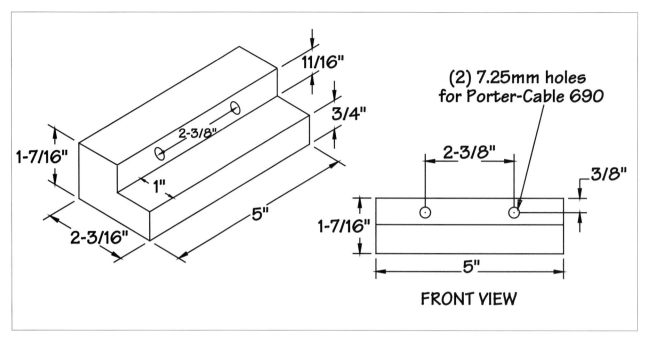

Figure 6-3B
Rabbeted rod-holding block.

Aluminum Setscrew Holding Plate

The ¼"-thick aluminum bar stock is for the setscrews. The rod-holding block will also be tapped, and their combined holding power will resist any effort to strip out the threads for the setscrews. The aluminum setscrew holding plate is fastened to the rod-holding block with three ¼-20x¾" flatheads; #12x¾" flathead sheet-metal screws are also acceptable.

STEP 1.   Take a length of ¼"x1" aluminum bar stock, and band saw or hacksaw to about 5". Sand to a net length of 5". Then, drill and countersink for three ¼-20 flathead machine screws (Figure 6-3C).

STEP 2.   Drill and tap the rod-holding block for the bar; the bar should be flush to the edge of the rod-holding block. Screw the plate to the rod-holding block.

STEP 3.   Now drill two centered ¹³⁄₆₄" holes through the sandwich intersecting the rod holes, and tap for ¼-20x½" cup point setscrews.

Auxiliary Fence

Using an edge guide for cuttings in the edge of stock will require an add-on fence. This auxiliary fence has two functions. It lengthens the guide surface by its own length, and it offers a "hideout" for the unused portion of the cutter. Without it you'll cut into the ½" platform and ruin it (Figure 6-6). My fence has been stylized, but the one you'll make works just as well.

STEP 1.   Cut a ⅝"x1⅞"x8" piece of hardwood.

STEP 2.   Load into the clamping template, and rout a ½"-deep by ⅞"-wide rabbet into its 1⅞" dimension (Figure 6-3D).

STEP 3   Drill a 1⅛" half-circle on the edge of

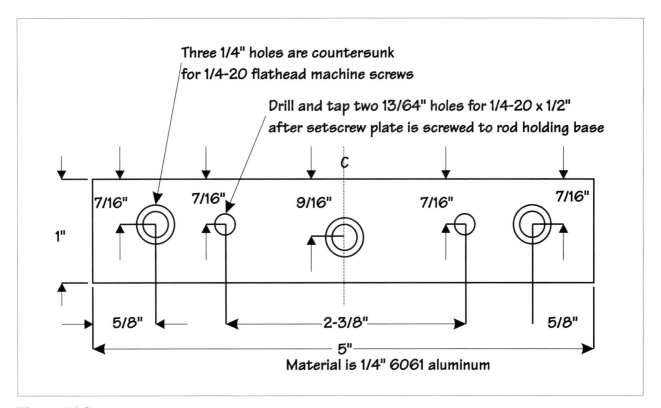

Three 1/4" holes are countersunk
for 1/4-20 flathead machine screws

Drill and tap two 13/64" holes for 1/4-20 x 1/2"
after setscrew plate is screwed to rod holding base

C

7/16"   7/16"   9/16"   7/16"   7/16"

1"

5/8"   2-3/8"   5/8"

5"
Material is 1/4" 6061 aluminum

Figure 6-3C
Aluminum setscrew holding plate.

Figure 6-5
If it weren't for the jig the edge guide is resting on, the very large rabbet in the rod-holding block would be hard to make. It often takes a jig to make a jig, and sometimes the jig itself is needed.

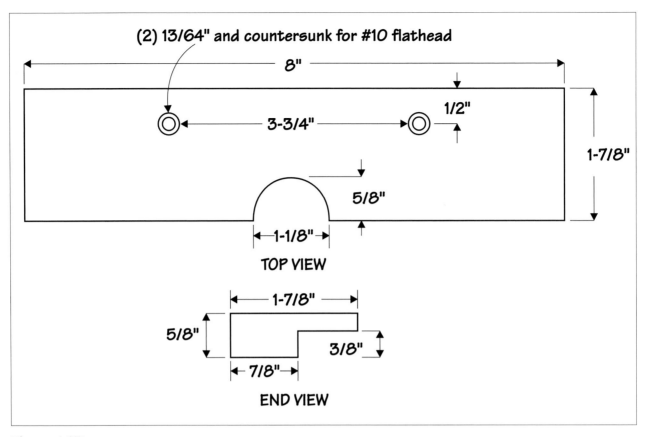

(2) 13/64" and countersunk for #10 flathead

8"

3-3/4"

1/2"

1-7/8"

5/8"

1-1/8"

TOP VIEW

1-7/8"

5/8"

3/8"

7/8"

END VIEW

Figure 6-3D
Hardwood auxiliary fence.

its long center line or rout the hide-out with a template and flush trim cutter (Figure 6-7).

STEP 4. Center the auxiliary fence on the platform, against its rabbet, and transfer the two-hole pretapped pattern onto it. Drill $^{13}\!/_{64}$" holes and countersink for 10-24x¾" flathead screws.

TWO CUTS WITH THE EDGE GUIDE

As designed, this edge guide is to be used in combination with my or your offset subbase. In this configuration, the offset base is rotated so that its grip knob is opposite the edge guide,

substantially reducing the usual handling problem associated with routing without one (Figure 6-1).

In this mode the auxiliary fence is positioned under the body (platform) of the edge guide to clear the thicker (in my case, 12mm) subbase.

A Wide Rabbet

Let's take a wide slice, say ¼"x¾", along the edge of a board ⅝" thick. First, take a light anti-climb score cut, and then finish the rabbet, paring away the stock as the router allows.

Set the north/south depth of cut to ¼" and the east/west edge guide depth to ⅛". Tighten all hardware, and pull and press the machine against the stock to verify it won't slip. Now

Figure 6-6
This cutout in the fence will hide more than half of a 1"-diameter cutter. You need this space to put the unused diameter of the cutter as you rout along the edges of stock.

Figure 6-7
Drill or rout out the cavity, as I did, with a template and trim-to-template cutter.

climb cut right to left. If you feel edgy about climb cutting, do indeed rout left to right; this light cut should not tear out.

Now set the guide so the cutter will reach ½" to 1" in board. For me, 1" is OK as I will pare the cut away and take it in multiple climb and anti-climb passes. Keep the router firmly on the substrate with the offset knob as any tipping will spoil the cut (Figure 6-8).

The Stopped Dado

For this inside cut we'll use the Bakelite round subbase, so reposition the auxiliary fence to the top surface of the body. We'll stop the cut with an edge guide stop. Position the cutter so it's coincident with your stop scribe line on the work with the router clamped down. Now rout left to right concentrating on firm edge to edge guide contact as any deviation will spoil the cut (Figure 6-9).

Figure 6-8
The score cut, just ⅛" wide, meets the wide cut, neither of which is torn out. Usually it is possible to prevent tear-out. However, sometimes it takes more time than it's worth to prevent it.

Figure 6-9
The left-to-right travel of the router is limited by the stop block. If accuracy is your goal, make a rabbeted stop like this one. All successive cuts will be exactly alike. This cut is said to be at risk, as any deviation of the guide from the stock will be copied in the dado.

CHAPTER SEVEN

End-Lapping and Two-Faced Tenoning Jig

This jig is a very simple clamp/template for cutting half-laps and two-faced tenons. It, like many others, is very job specific so you won't be using it everyday. It is small, however, so storing it with its "mother" template will be to particular advantage (Figures 7-1, 7-2).

My first approximation to this jig was in *Router Joinery Handbook*. I regard jigmaking and use as evolutionary; consequently, this model has been upgraded. The changes include a slightly larger window to allow more freedom for the cutter, more MDF surface area for the router, a fence with a little slop built into it for 90° calibration, and the use of only two fasteners, which are centered directly under the clamp flanges where all the stress is.

There are no moving parts to the jig. The work is positioned against the fence, clamped and advanced into the window an amount equal to the length of tenon or lap. A large subbase is

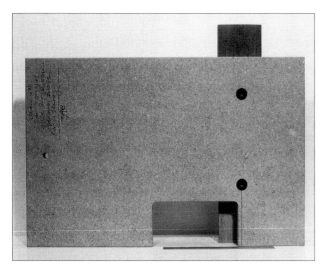

Figure 7-1
This is the work side of the jig. There is nothing in the pathway of the router.

Figure 7-2
The underside of the template (with the rear clamp off) showing the adjuster nut/bolt. This hole is ²¹⁄₆₄" *and the screw is* ⁵⁄₁₆" *in diameter, so there is about* ⁺⁄.007" *of adjustment.*

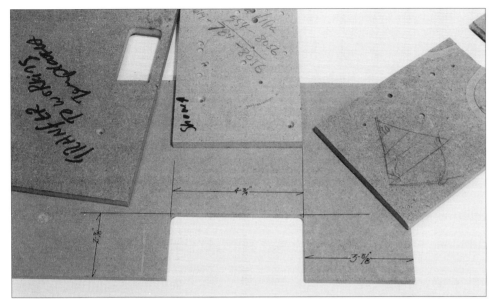

Figure 7-3

Often in jigmaking you need the very thing you're making to make it! Not in this case; you fabricate your own template simply by clamping or screwing down sections of template where needed.

necessary and so is a fixed-base or plunge router. The wide subbase is to ensure against an accidental slip into the window. The router bit must be able to reach any point within the cutout without the base slipping off any edge. We'll make a ⅜"-thick fiberboard subbase for this jig. But first let's make the jig and a template to make the cutout/window.

THE WINDOW/CUTOUT TEMPLATE

This template will make it easier for you to cut the window in the jig, and you can use it to true up the window in the event of an accident or undue wear and tear. The template-jig is designed for material up to 1½" thick with the toggle clamps, or for any rational thickness with C-clamps, with widths to 3½" and any lengths. The maximum tenon length of 2⅜" and the depth of cut are limited only by the flute length of the cutter; ½"- to ¾"-deep cuts are easily attainable. Study the design and if the cutout template does not meet your needs, make the changes to the window/cutout template now.

STEP 1.   Cut a ⅜"-thick piece of MDF to an approximately 6"x12" rectangle.

STEP 2.   Block out an area 2⅜"x4¾"about 3⅝" from one end (see Figure 7-3) with ¼", ⅜" or ½" MDF.

STEP 3.   Now jigsaw out the waste and rout to the edge of your clamped-down temporary template stock.

THE JIG TEMPLATE

STEP 1.   Cut a 10"x15½" rectangle of ¾" MDF.

STEP 2.   Jig or band saw out the window cutout within ⅛" or so of a tracing (coincident) of the template above.

STEP 3.   Clamp the template to the jig and rout to pattern with a pattern bit at least ¾" long.

STEP 4.   Drill two ⁵⁄₁₆" holes as shown in the drawing (Figure 7-4B), and lightly chamfer all edges of the jig.

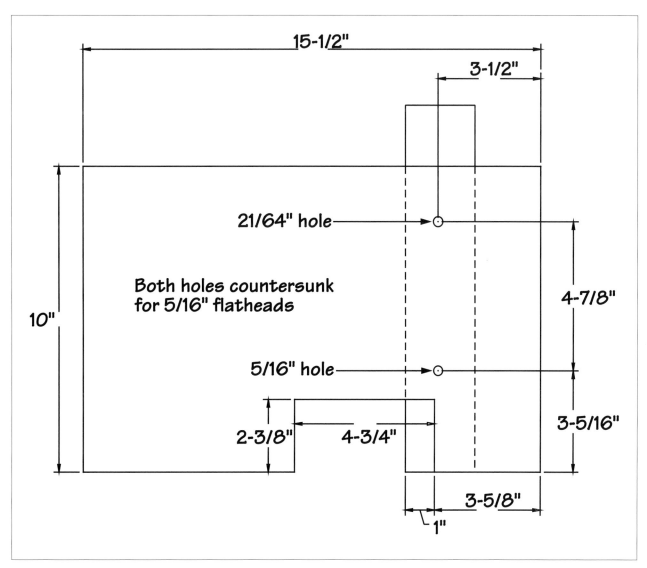

Figure 7-4A

Template jig platform.

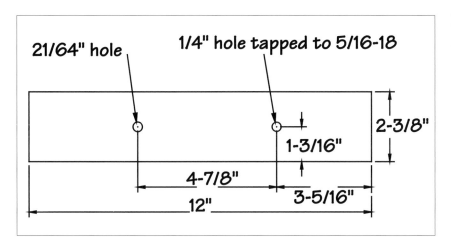

Figure 7-4B

Fence showing size and holes.

The Fence

The fence should be made of very stable, straight 1"-thick hardwood, Jatoba in my case. Not only does your referencing depend on this stick, but two 500-pound clamps will be bolted to it, so it must be strong, stable and straight.

STEP 1.　Joint, plane and chop your fence into a 1"x2⅜"x12" rectangle.

STEP 2.　Use a square and rule to position the fence 1" inside the cutout and flush with the edge of the jig (Figure 7-5).

STEP 3.　Once in that position, transfer punch the two-hole pattern from the jig onto the fence. Drill a ¼" hole nearest the cutout, and tap it with a ⁵⁄₁₆-18 tap. Drill the other hole to ²¹⁄₆₄".

STEP 4.　Counterbore the ²¹⁄₆₄" hole with a ⅞" counterbore, such as a W.L. Fuller B610, to a depth of ⅜".

STEP 5.　Now center the four-hole bolt pattern for 225-U toggle clamps directly around these ⁵⁄₁₆" bolt holes (see Figure 7-4B for details), and tap them for ¼-20x¾" buttonheads.

The Subbase

Now let's make a large square ⅜"-thick MDF subbase for your router with a 2" cutter hole.

STEP 1.　Cut a 9¼" square piece of ⅜" MDF and mark its center. Center your base casting screw hole pattern around the center of the square. You may want to move the center hole over 1" or so as this will allow more router overhang stability.

Note: Nearly every router maker has different screws, holes and hole patterns for their base casting to subbase connection. To match them to any degree takes machine shop equipment and know-how. For a satisfactory transfer, use the base plate simply as a drill hole template and oversize the holes by at least one size (.0015" to .002" larger). Pan head screws will also help.

Figure 7-5
To square up this fence you need three hands or three clamps and two hands. Hands are handy. Clamp the template, clamp the reference surface in the cutout, and square the stick to the reference edge.

Figure 7-6

Lightly climb-cut a ¹⁄₁₆" score-cut around the perimeter of the lap starting at the right hand corner. This prevents any and all tear-out. This is one of the lowest-risk (to the work), highest-quality router cuts I know of. The only way to screw this up is by missing the correct depth of cut.

Figure 7-7

Some applications of the connections include: seat frames, light cabinet doors, frames for drawer dividers, cabinet backs and face frames.

Assembly and Calibration

STEP 1.   Insert ⁵⁄₁₆-18x1¾" flathead screws through the template into the fence. Use a ⅞"x⁵⁄₁₆" hole washer and ⁵⁄₁₆-18 nut in the counterbore. The fence bolt is slightly sloppy in this hole. Use a square referenced from the 4¾" edge of the cutout to bring the fence into a 90° corner, and tighten up the screws (Figure 7-5).

MAKING AN END HALF LAP

The lap is a relatively easy task, and you should be able to rout the first one square and with no tear-out. As with all router joinery, particular attention must be paid to material preparation.

STEP 1.   Prepare your stock in the usual way, and knife a line across the stock at the shoulder for the lap.

STEP 2.   Set the toggle clamps to hold the work, and set the knife line even with the working edge of the template. Clamp the jig to your bench.

STEP 3.   For cuts less than ½" deep, use PRC TA-170 shank bearing trimmers. For equal-thickness laps, set the depth of cut to one-half thickness. Take an ⅛" trip around the perimeter of the lap (Figure 7-6), so the cleanup cuts won't tear out. Though the flute length of the TA-170 is ½", don't take much more than a ³⁄₁₆" pass. A plunge router is probably the better tool for cuts over ¼" deep.

STEP 4.   Use a marking gauge (as a stop) to set the projection of the work into the cutout. Flip the work over if you are making two-faced tenons, and use the marking gauge to reposition the work (Figure 7-7).

CHAPTER EIGHT

The Router Horse and 90° Template

Routing is most frequently done on individual furniture and cabinet parts. There are, of course, occasions when the entire project gets routed after assembly, but as a rule, routing is done on individual and relatively small workpieces. When I do seminars and field demonstrations, I usually rout examples of mortises, tenons, laps and template cuttings on stock less than 18" long and 6" wide. Moreover, the furniture I make rarely calls for stock more than 6' long. A full-size bench, therefore, is just plain unnecessary for hand routings. A big bench is critical for panel routing, assembly and a zillion other tasks, but not for the majority of router work.

Years ago I invented a 7' router beam (Figure 8-1) 6½" wide that rested approximately 40" from the floor. At that time I did most of my routing by hand and not much at all on the router table. After making many examples of furniture on the beam, it became clear that the 7' dimension was seldom necessary and often an

Figure 8-1
This triangulated 6½"-wide beam was my first experiment in a router-specific workbench. I designed a 7" overhang on one end. The beam is 40" high.

Figure 8-2
These clamp knobs fix the beam to the router table by screwing into T-nuts under the table.

annoyance. The model in this chapter has been modified substantially from the embryo; it's very easy to make, very handy, storable and can be used almost as frequently as the 7' model. The important thing to remember here is that a lot of hand routings are done on short, narrow boards; a narrow beam is easier to clamp to, and you have the option of working on either side. On a big bench this is usually not the case.

A 6½"x34" beam, although quite short and narrow, can easily support a 10"-wide by 50"-long board since only 8" would be hanging off each end and 1¾" off each side. If you make your beam like mine, you will not only be pleasantly surprised at how easy ordinary routing can be, you will also find that the paneled end of the fixture really makes difficult and tricky end cuts, such as sliding dovetails, a snap.

HORSE SENSE

This beam is only 6½" high, so you'll need to place and clamp it to an existing surface. I "clamp-knob" mine atop the router table which is heavy enough to be stable (Figure 8-2). The combined height puts the surface at 42½". I

Figure 8-3
I welded the fixed end of this C-clamp to a ¼"-thick piece of steel and screwed it to the underside of the beam so it only takes one hand to operate.

Figure 8-4
These steel cross dowels are great for knockdown assembly.

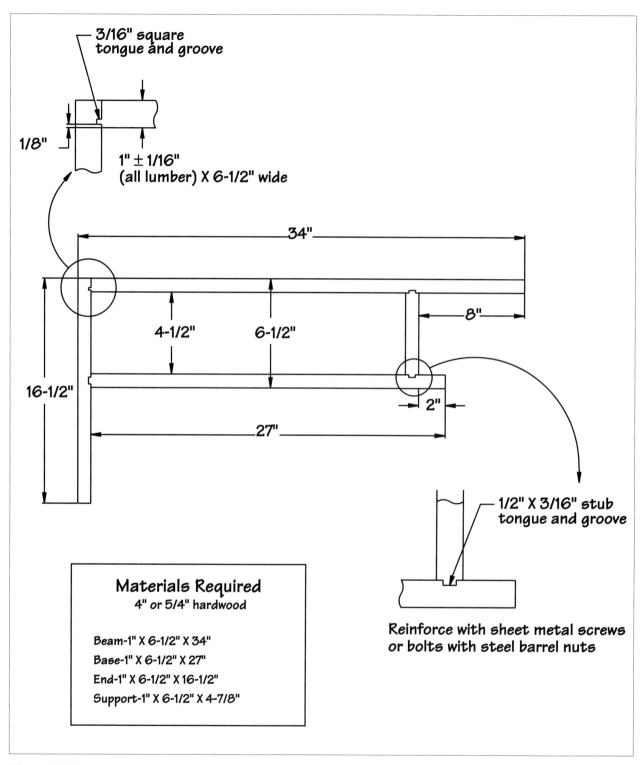

**3/16" square
tongue and groove**

1/8"

1" ± 1/16"
(all lumber) X 6-1/2" wide

34"

4-1/2"   6-1/2"

8"

16-1/2"

2"

27"

Materials Required
4" or 5/4" hardwood

Beam-1" X 6-1/2" X 34"
Base-1" X 6-1/2" X 27"
End-1" X 6-1/2" X 16-1/2"
Support-1" X 6-1/2" X 4-7/8"

1/2" X 3/16" stub
tongue and groove

**Reinforce with sheet metal screws
or bolts with steel barrel nuts**

Figure 8-5A
The router horse.

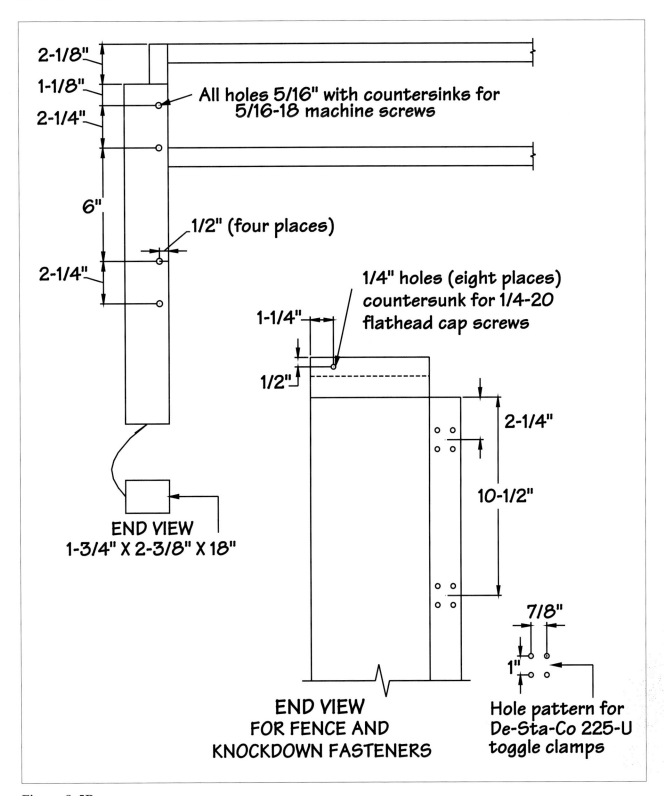

2-1/8"

1-1/8"

2-1/4"

All holes 5/16" with countersinks for 5/16-18 machine screws

6"

1/2" (four places)

2-1/4"

1/4" holes (eight places) countersunk for 1/4-20 flathead cap screws

1-1/4"

1/2"

END VIEW
1-3/4" X 2-3/8" X 18"

2-1/4"

10-1/2"

END VIEW
FOR FENCE AND
KNOCKDOWN FASTENERS

7/8"

1"

Hole pattern for De-Sta-Co 225-U toggle clamps

Figure 8-5B

Fastener layout.

Figure 8-5C
Cross-bolt locations and dimensions.

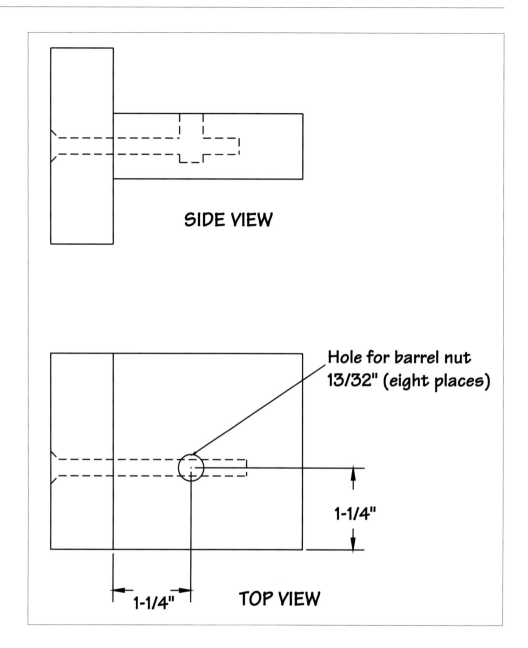

SIDE VIEW

Hole for barrel nut
13/32" (eight places)

1-1/4"

1-1/4"   TOP VIEW

mounted a Jorgensen deep-throat (no. 175) C-clamp on it (Figure 8-3). I had a predrilled ¼"x1"x4" steel plate welded to the fixed end so I could screw it permanently in place. The best place to locate it is uncertain; you'll have to experiment.

You'll need about 7' of 6½"-wide 5/4 material to make the horse. I used walnut, but beech, maple, birch and ash are also quite suitable. Select the straightest boards for the best resistance to distortion. Mill the stock to about 1". I

used knockdown open joinery reinforced with steel cross dowels for the assembly (Figure 8-4). I chose the knockdown assembly for strength and ease of disassembly should I want to repair or modify it.

I designed an 8" overhang into the jig for easy clamping of templates and longer work (see Figure 8-5A). The other two feet of the underside of the beam are essentially clear of all clamp obstacles, so a workpiece can be clamped anywhere on either side of the jig. The top also has a 1⅛" hole in it, so a router or jigsaw even with its cutter extended can rest flat (subbase down) over the hole.

A fence with toggle clamps is situated on the edge of the end panel 2⅛" below the work surface; it must be square to the top. I use it to reference cuts that are done on stock clamped vertically, such as sliding dovetails, tenons, and cross-grain slots on narrow panels (Figure 8-6).

MAKING THE HORSE

STEP 1.   Joint, plane and cut the panels as indicated in drawing (Figure 8-5A).

STEP 2.   Cut a ³⁄₁₆"-square slot in the end panel as shown and three ³⁄₁₆"-deep by ½"-wide dadoes where indicated.

STEP 3.   Form the matching tongues on the support and base.

STEP 4.   Now assemble and clamp. Drill through the assembly on the center line of each joint to a depth of 2⅝" with a ¼" drill.

STEP 5.   Disassemble and drill ¹³⁄₃₂" blind holes on the center lines of the holes in step 4, 1¼" from the joint shoulders on the support, base and beam. Use Bruss CD03 cross dowels and ¼-20x2½" flathead Allen machine screws.

THE FENCE

An important feature of the fixture is its ability to hold and index the work on-end (vertically). The fence on the end panel has the clamps to hold the work and it's at a right angle to the work surface, so any straight stick clamped to it will be automatically indexed for square cuts. There's a lot of stress on this component and the edge of the panel it's fastened to.

Figure 8-6
This fence has the dual function of indexing and holding work on end.

In fact, I thought I might split the panel if the clamps were fully loaded (De-Sta-Co 225-U clamps have a 500-pound load rating!). Fortunately, this hasn't happened, but if it does, I have a strategy to remedy it. I'll join and bolt a stick to both the reference surface of the fence and the panel like an outside corner brace.

Anyway, the fence is quite stout and well secured with four ⁵⁄₁₆-18x3" cap screws threaded into the edge grain of the vertical panel (Figure 8-6). Make the fence from something strong like oak or walnut.

INSTALLING CROSS DOWELS

Steel cross dowels and bolts have been around for a long time. They are the most effective knockdown fasteners I know of. They are quite straightforward in nature, but their installation can be tricky. A pilot hole and countersink are required in the first piece of wood to be joined, and the same pilot hole continues in the second workpiece. The second workpiece also requires a mortise to accommodate the cross dowel, and this mortise must intersect the pilot hole—the intersecting hole must be smack on the center line of the pilot hole for the assembly to work.

The pilot holes are bored with little problem, especially if the workpieces can be clamped together to ensure proper registration. The hole for the cross dowel is also easy to drill, but locating exactly where to drill presents the problem. How do you find the center line of a hole you can't see? A few simple tools will help: a sliding T-bevel, a block of wood, a writing pen and a couple of transfer punches.

I use a Faber-Castell .2mm Uni-ball pen. It draws about a .01" to .012" line on wood. Select a transfer punch that matches the pilot hole, which happens to be ¼" in my case. After drilling your pilot holes, insert the transfer punch in the hole of the workpiece that receives the cross dowel, and clamp the workpiece down. Gently clamp a block of wood, thicker than the workpiece, butted against the transfer punch. Set the blade of the T-bevel against the wood block, with the handle against the end of the workpiece, to establish the true angle (Figure 8-7). It would be 90° if you drilled perfectly, but the angle is probably off by a couple of degrees.

Now, place a ⁹⁄₆₄" transfer punch or drill

shank between the block and the blade while keeping the T-bevel's handle against the end of the workpiece. Draw a pen line along the workpiece, letting the blade of the T-bevel guide your pen. The ⁹⁄₆₄" punch transfers the scribe line one pilot hole radius from the edge of the hole, so your pen line ends up, for all practical purposes, centered along the length of the pilot hole (Figure 8-8).

The hole for the cross dowel can be drilled anywhere on the center of the line, but for maximum strength the hole should be located so that the cross dowel runs through the entire diameter of the bolt. Cross dowels can vary in diameter from machine shop to machine shop, so measure them before drilling. Allow ¹⁄₆₄" or less slop for the dowel. I used 82°, ¼-20x2½" alloy flathead, Allen-driven cap screws for my assembly (a semistandard hardware item). The cross dowels I used were ¾" long with matching ¼-20 threaded holes (Bruss CD05 fasteners, see Sources).

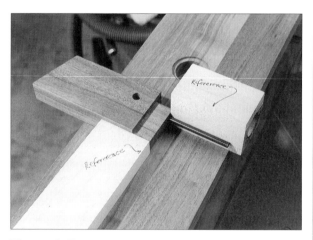

Figure 8-7
Two reference surfaces are needed to fix the angle of the T-bevel. The end of the stock and a stick against a punch in the hole provide those surfaces.

INSTALLING CROSS DOWELS CONTINUED

To find the center line to locate a cross dowel, do the following:

1. Insert the proper-sized transfer punch. Begin by setting the angle with the T-bevel's blade against the wood block and the handle against the end of the second workpiece.

2. Offset the blade ⁹⁄₆₄" with the drill rod— this will place the scribed line very near the actual center line.

3. Drill the hole for the cross dowel at the appropriate location along the marked center line.

Note: A knife line or sharp, hard pencil scribe is essentially invisible when drawn along the grain of many woods, hence the need for a pen.

Figure 8-8
Using a punch as a spacer, reposition the blade for an ink line coincident with the center of the hole. Clamp the work and the reference stick down.

STEP 1. Cut and square up a 1¾"x2⅜"x18" length of prime straight-grained material from an old-growth stand.

STEP 2. Drill and countersink as shown.

STEP 3. Position the fence 2⅛" below the top and flush to the edge of the panel and transfer punch the hole pattern onto the edge.

STEP 4. Drill and tap the edge of the panel.

Assembly

If you're lucky, and your milling was good and the weather agreeable, your work may be square on assembly. Bolt the unit together, but don't drive the screws home like tractor wheel lug nuts. Just bring the pieces together and add maybe ¹⁄₁₆ of a turn. Screw on the fence and toggle clamps.

Calibration

To get square cuts the fence has to be square to the top and any 90° template has to be square to the end of the fixture. There is no easy fix if the unit is out of square. It's scrape, shim and sand, all unpleasantries to be sure.

Squaring the End Panel to the Surface

The fence can only be shimmed if out of square. You can apply layers of tape where the work rests and that will help a lot. If the fence is way out, you should mount it on the face of the panel and allow it to pivot, square it, then bolt it in place.

Squaring the Template to the Panel

End cuts (vertically held work) require the assistance of a template. Fortunately, this most critical proposition is easily accounted for. Even if

Figure 8-9

Use a .002" feeler gauge between your template and the reference surface. Any deviation here will be expressed as a taper on your end cuttings.

Figure 8-10

Locating the template is a direct measurement to the end of the stock. One side of the cut of a bearing-guided cutter will be essentially parallel and next to the template.

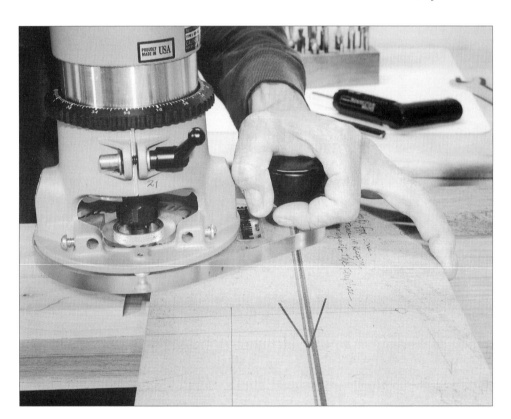

Figure 8-11

With my fingers pulled over the left edge of the template, I'm sure to keep the collar against the right side. This also helps keep the machine flat on the template. Let the knob track the black line parallel to the edge. This keeps the same section (radian) of the collar always against the template.

the reference edge of the jig is "out" you can adjust the work edge of the template to accommodate.

STEP 1. Clamp some metal or fiberboard above and across the end panel (Figure 8-9).

STEP 2. With a square, check the angle of the jig and fiberboard. If it isn't 90° and your 90° template is, you'll have to shave away some template so its edge is exactly parallel with the end panel lest your tenons and other end cuts will taper.

USING THE ROUTER HORSE

Cutting a Dado

A dado can be cut with a 90° template just by clamping it down on the work with its work edge some prescribed distance from the end of the stock (Figures 8-10, 8-11). Use an offset sub-base with a collar attached for best results.

Figure 8-12

Let the template hang over the edge to reference the work flush to the top. Sometimes I'll use a third clamp to help flatten and hold the work.

Cutting Cross-Grain Slots

On occasion you may have the need for a cross-grain slot for a drawer back or other assembly. For this operation:

STEP 1.   Position the work on the end panel, flush to the top, and clamp it in place (Figure 8-12).

STEP 2.   Now, with a cutter (e.g., ¼"x³⁄₁₆" deep) like the Whiteside 2902, a fixed-base router and offset subbase, set the depth of cut.

STEP 3.   Rout the slot across the grain (Figure 8-13).

Figure 8-13

A groover (a.k.a. face inlay or slotter bit), like this Whiteside MC 2902, is the best type of tool for a slot like this.

Figure 8-14

I took this cut in two stages. The second cut was stopped. Both cutting tools are shown. One of them has a bearing larger than the bit diameter.

Cutting Two-Faced Tenons

It's best, but not essential, to cut the faces of the tenon at one vertical depth. If you'd like to take multiple passes on deep cuts, reposition the template, don't change the cutter height.

STEP 1.   Use a collar and offset subbase for safety and set the cutter height to its finish depth.

STEP 2.   Clamp a 90° template at the prescribed distance from the face of the stock to yield the desired shoulder width. For flush trimming bearing-guided tools, the distance is essentially equal to the shoulder (Figure 8-14). For long (longer than 1") tenons with wide shoulders, consider using two routers, letting the first router cut at least half the swath. Rout the shoulder.

STEP 3.   Reposition the work (180°) flush against the underside of the template, clamp, and rout (in two stages if necessary).

CHAPTER NINE

The Four-Faced Tenon Making Jig

Tenons are always produced from outside cuttings, such as those from band, radial, table or back saws. They can also be planed or chiseled. There are many ways to cut them, each with its own advantages, limitations and characteristic results. This jig presents the fewest compromises and, with nice sharp cutters, the best results (Figure 9-1).

As just mentioned, there are a lot of ways to cut tenons, but I have yet to see a nonproduction process produce tenons as pretty, as exact and as easy as the ones you'll be making with

my tenoner/jig (Figure 9-2). The jig is the heart of the process, but a plunge router, a few rabbet bits and a couple of bearings are also needed. The jig is an MDF platform/holder. The platform supports the router, which has a ski subbase on it to keep it from tipping into the window where the workpiece is accessed. The work-holding and indexing functions of the jig are met with an MDF panel and fence perpendicular to this platform (Figures 9-3A, B). The tenon is formed by one or several trips around the work with a bearing-piloted rabbet bit. The lateral

Figure 9-1
These tenons are really easy to make and take less than a minute to index, position and rout.

Figure 9-2

The fence, either panel or the workpiece can be clamped in the vise or on your bench beam. Be sure it's well secured before routing.

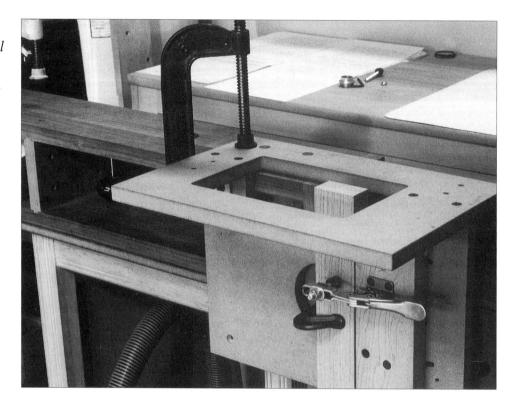

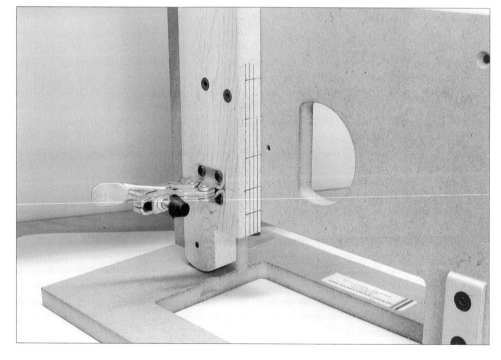

Figure 9-3A

The vertical panel and the fence provide the nest for the work-piece. I use a toggle clamp with a C-clamp to secure the work in the jig.

(east/west) depth of cut is determined by the cutter diameter and bearing, and the vertical (north/south) depth of cut is determined by your plunging depth. The whole affair is held fast either by the work or by clamping the fence in a vise.

The jig is small and portable. It can be made as sophisticated as you like, or it can function

Figure 9-3B
The work is clamped on a penny. The window in the vertical panel is for more clamping access.

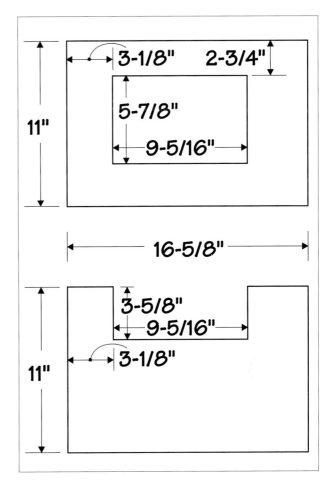

Figure 9-4A
Jig construction details.

quite well even if you cobble it together with a jigsaw, drywall screws and glue. My jig has been carefully template-routed, joined and machine screwed together. Jigs are evolutionary: The first one is usually an approximation; as your skills improve, so do your jigs. Let this first one be a learning experience and make the next one sweeter. Plan on cutting the windows out with a jigsaw or hand saw, and do, by all means, use #8 or #10 drywall screws to hold it together.

This jig is my invention, and, as of February 1999, I'm the only one making them. If you're unwilling, unable or just too impatient to make one of my tenoners, you can order one from me

(see Sources).

Before starting out, read this entire section so you thoroughly understand the construction and just where you should make changes if you'd like to tenon larger stock. The nominal holding capacity of my jig is for stock up to 2¼"-thick, 6"-wide and any length. There are off-the-shelf cutters and arbors to produce four-faced centered tenons with shoulders up to ⁹⁄₁₆" and lengths to 2½" (see Using the Tenoner, step 4).

Figure 9-4B

Joinery details.

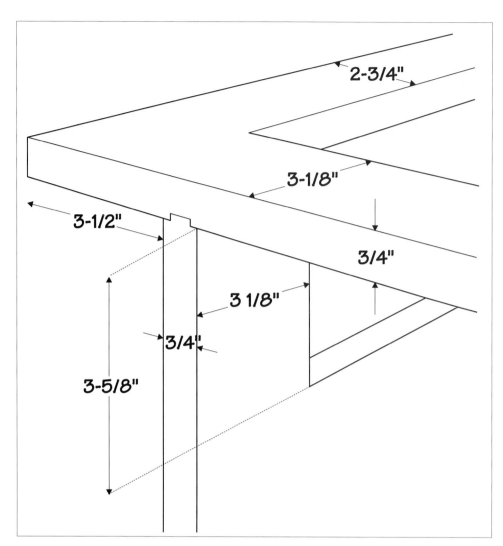

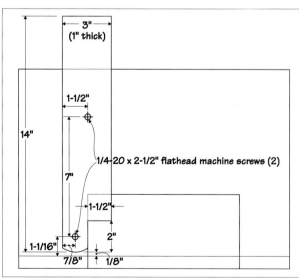

Figure 9-6

The fence and its location on the panel with screws.

MAKING THE JIG FOR 90° USE

STEP 1. Cut two pieces of MDF to 11"x16⅝".

STEP 2. Cut windows in the panels as shown (Figure 9-4A). They needn't be precise, because they are merely access windows. If the stock you plan to tenon is larger than 2¼"x6", add the equivalent amount (in inches) to the window and panel dimensions, respectively (i.e., for stock over the 6" dimension, add to the long dimension of the window and panel).

STEP 3. Screw and/or tongue-and-groove the

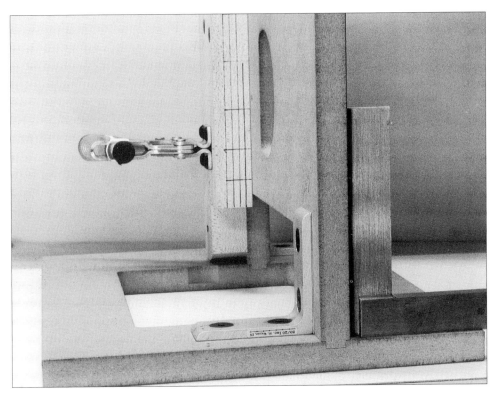

Figure 9-5

These panels must be at 90°. You may have to shim the corner braces to achieve a right angle. Do whatever it takes; this is the one critical point.

Figure 9-7

Square the fence to the top panel as shown and clamp it in place. Use the hole in the fence as a guide to locate the hole to be drilled in the panel. Drill a ⁵⁄₁₆" hole in the panel. I have a third screw in mine for more security. (I have a transfer punch in the hole.)

panels together so the center line of the vertical panel is 3⅞" from the edge of the horizontal panel, thus lining up the windows.

STEP 4.   Reinforce as necessary with shop-made corner braces or machined right-angle aluminum or steel brackets. These panels must be at right angles (Figure 9-5).

STEP 5.   Now make the fence from a piece of hardwood 1¼"x3½"x14". Notch it as shown in the drawing (Figure 9-6) and fasten it to the panel with a ¼-20x2½" machine screw and nut. Put a second screw 7" away from this one.

STEP 6. Before drilling the hole in the panel for the second screw, square the fence to the top (Figure 9-7). This hole is sloppy so you can adjust the fence to exactly 90° before tightening the nut. **Caution:** The fence should always be well secured. Use three screws if necessary. If the fence should ever rotate while tenoning, you will spoil the work and perhaps have an accident. Double-check the security of the fence before each use.

STEP 7. Install a De-Sta-Co 225-U toggle clamp, centered, approximately 3½" from the top of the fence (1½" down from the notch). Use four #12x1¼" pan head sheet-metal screws to fasten the fence.

USING THE TENONER

STEP 1. Upend the tenoner on your workbench.

STEP 2. Place a penny against the fence and set the toggle clamp. Always use an additional C-clamp to clamp the work in the jig (Figure 9-3B).

STEP 3. Invert the jig and secure in a vise (Figure 9-2). Make sure your work is held securely in the vise. Test your setup by pulling the jig back and forth before routing. When you're routing you will add 15 to 20 pounds of weight and force to the system. If anything should slip, you could spoil the work or perhaps lose your balance. The jig is very safe: I've made hundreds of perfect tenons without any accidents. Knowing these few things beforehand should prepare you for any mishaps.

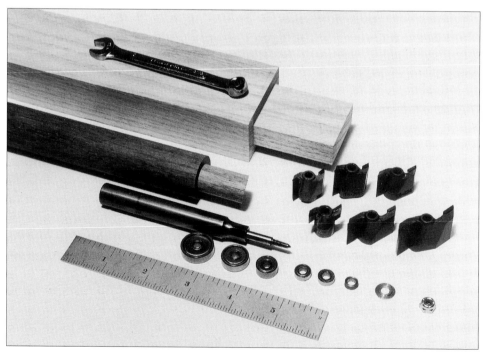

Figure 9-8
This is the longest arbor I know of (4⅜"). PRC makes four rabbet bits and eight groovers for this arbor. With 1" in the collet you can make a 3"-long tenon.

Figure 9-9

The complete setup. The work is indexed, secured and one penny's thickness lower than the work surface. The whole affair is clamped in the vise or on your beam, and the plunge router has a ski on it big enough that it'll span the window under all conditions.

Figure 9-10

During your final pass (for each depth of cut) make sure the bearing rolls on the faces of the stock to be routed. The surface of the work is the reference surface for the bearing. If you skip a spot, you can't go back and cut it again (at a new depth) because the bearing will be rolling on the cheek, a nonreference surface.

STEP 4. Collet up the rabbet bit and bearing that match your shoulder requirements. Use PRC arbor TA-160-XL and TA-222 (⅛"), TA-224 (¼"), TA-222 (⅜") or TA-228 rabbet bits for the appropriate shoulder (Figure 9-8). Contact PRC (800-237-8613) for cutter and bearing specifics and set the depth to one-half the cutter height. Use a plunge router with a wide platform subbase that always straddles the window (Figure 9-9).

STEP 5. Rout around the end of the work counterclockwise, finishing with the bearing against each face of the board. If only one, two or three faces are required, keep the cutter off the appropriate face(s). Lower the cutter one-fourth to one-half flute length, rout, and repeat to the maximum depth (Figure 9-10). If there should be any tear-out, try to climb cut, but take shallow cuts (⅜" or less deep).

CHAPTER TEN
The Circle-Cutting Subbase

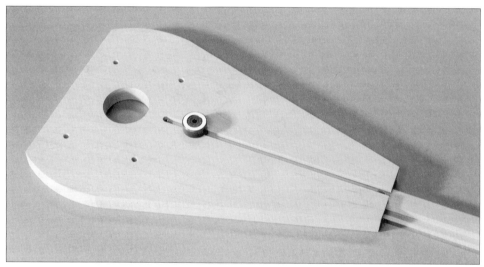

Figure 10-1
This is the router side of the jig. It has been styled. The big washer and cap screw keep the pivot arm firmly in place.

Circle cutting has been a jig or band saw process essentially because of efficiency not accuracy. A good band saw jig is much faster than a router, especially on thick stock. However, I'm one who would rather be skilled at making jigs and furniture than master a technique-sensitive process like band sawing circles. Not only does the band saw require a jig and lots of practice to do well, but you can't make a precise circle with one, nor will the edges be good enough for template use.

The jig you'll make will cut to .001". The work will be round. Unlike the cuttings with a band saw, both the inside and outside circles will be smooth and useful for a full 360°. The cuttings will be messier and slower but precise and suitable for template use.

Since the router is always supported by the work and the cuts have to be done in stages, the plunge router is the obvious choice to make circles with. The circle subbase will eventually be drilled for your favorite plunger.

The plan of attack is as follows: First you'll prepare a couple of planks. To do this, take the planks to the router table for slotting and rabbeting, then drill them for your router. The pivoting arm, separate from the base, should be made on your clamp template. You'll notice I said planks, not plank. I think there is some risk to the work in slotting, so you can use one for setup and the other for yourself. If the setup plank finishes up without any errors, dress it up a little and give it to a friend with a router like yours.

THE ROUTER BASE BODY

My circle subbase is designed for the DeWalt 621 (Figures 10-1, 10-2). The act of cutting circles traps the chip in the cutter pathway. The 621 with its integral dust collection will exhaust the chip like no other, hence my choice for a circle-cutting router. A reasonable base-plate width for this tool is 7⅜". The DeWalt 621 base is not symmetrical to the cutter, so the 7⅜" dimension is related more to ergonomics and necessity rather than symmetry. The majority of plunge routers, however, are symmetrical, so first determine a reasonable diameter for your tool before cutting this plank. Add about ⅛" to the diameter of your router to arrive at the correct width.

Cut the plank 11½" to 12" long, and style the blank as desired. My tool is radiused and truncated to roughly match the shape of the router and tapers to 2¼". Keep the blank as a rectangle, however, until you've completed the following machine work.

STEP 1.   Square up and mill your plank to ⅝".

STEP 2.   Mark the short center line of the rectangle and adjust the router table fence so the cutter will be on this center.

STEP 3.   Position a stop so that the cutter diameter travel of a ¼" bit is limited to about 1½" from the center of the cutter hole in the blank. The three cuttings to receive the slide are next.

I decided on three because the slide will interlock with the base with more purchase if it is rabbeted. I do think, however, that a ¼"x1" piece of aluminum will work as well if not better. So you may want to opt for metal or maybe even a ¼"- to ⅜"-thick blade of wood instead of this rabbeted blade (Figure 10-3). The routing exercise could, of course, be time well spent (for the rabbeting), but do indeed consider a simplification here.

STEP 4.　For best results use three different cutters, ¼", ⅝" and 1⅛" diameters, each to be used for only one diameter. Rout to ³⁄₁₆" with a 1⅛" tool, then to ⁹⁄₃₂" with the ⅝" cutter and through with the ¼" (Figure 10-4).

STEP 5.　Now drill the holes for your router. Either transfer the hole pattern from your router base plate or contact Woodhaven (see Sources) for their hole-locating templates for your particular router. A 1⅜" to 1⅝" cutter hole is a good size for cutter visibility and chip ejection.

STEP 6.　Radius and taper the shape of your plate if desired. It matters little, however, because the jig (while in rotation) is just as likely to hit an obstacle, such as a clamp, whether it's a rectangle or a triangle.

Making the Pivot Arm

Having 8" of slot milled into the base plate offers a lot of continuous adjustability, but you need more length. So let's make several pivot arms of various lengths. You can lash them together, if desired, rather than making one very long arm.

Figure 10-3

The blade articulates well with the double rabbet. It won't slip.

STEP 1. Mill a length of hardwood to a thickness that will fit the 1⅛" excavation in your blank. It should slide without slop, a slip fit.

STEP 2. Now joint both edges and band saw ½"-thick sticks off the board and plane to about ¹⁵⁄₃₂". It is important that the pivot arm (slide) is equal or less in thickness than the combined depth of the 1⅛"- and ⅝"-wide cuts in the blank.

STEP 3. Round the ends of the slide to nest in the ⅝" radius in the blank or chop the corners of the radius square.

STEP 4. Drill one ¼" pivot hole centered about ½" from either end and a ¹³⁄₆₄" hole, tapped to ¼-20, for the fastener. Drill other holes as necessary to fasten one arm to another to create one long pivot arm.

STEP 5. Now dig out your clamp template and clamp the slide to the template with about ⁵⁄₁₆" beyond the edge. Rabbet both sides of the slide, ¼" east/west and ⁹⁄₃₂" north/south (Figure 10-5). Finally, assemble the pivot

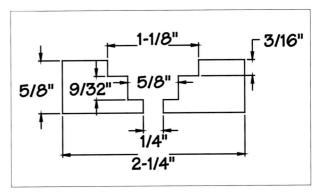

Figure 10-4
Cross section of rabbeting for pivot blade.

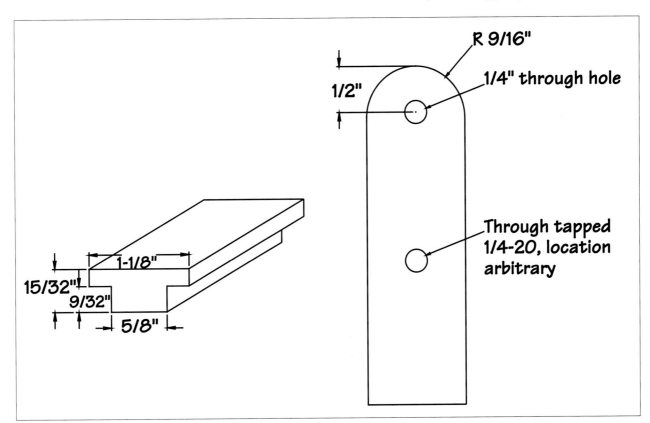

Figure 10-5
Pivot arm.

Figure 10-6

This measurement minus the cutter diameter, minus half the pivot pin (⅛") is equal to the disk radius of the work. The minimum disk diameter for my jig, with a ½"-diameter cutter is about 2½".

arm to the jig using the Reid Tool flat-foot JFF 19304 (see Sources) as a washer and a ¼-20x1" flathead socket cap screw.

THE NATURE OF DISKS AND ROUND HOLES

Whether you're going to produce an inside (concave) or outside (convex) radius on the work, it is less risky to the work to use a template. You can make all your mistakes on the template, preview, and make all critical measurements and fittings on cheap template stock; it's worth the extra step. Moreover, there's no need to bore a pivot hole in the work, since you can simply clamp the work to the template and use flush-trim pattern bits to trim the work even with the template.

USING THE JIG

As suggested, a template should be made first. To make a template, select a generous piece of MDF that you can clamp down outside the diameter of the circle you're cutting. One of the best cutters for this excavation is Jesada 611-564; it's a solid chunk of carbide welded into the end of a ½" shank, and as such it won't flex.

STEP 1.   To make a disk, insert a ¼" pin in the slide and measure to the cutter. The radius of the disk being cut is equal to the distance between the pin and the cutter plus the radius of the pin. Adjust the slide accordingly (Figure 10-6).

STEP 2.   Bore a through ¼" hole in the MDF and adjust the router to cut slightly less than halfway through. Make the circle cut; you will be pleasantly surprised if you have the vacuum attached and running on the DeWalt 621.

STEP 3.   Turn the fiberboard over and rout without changing the depth of cut. A thin web of MDF remains. Break the disk out of the MDF or use a jigsaw to cut through the web. Clean up the break with a laminate flush-trim bit such as a PRC TA-170 (Figure 10-7).

STEP 4.   Clamp the disk to your work and jigsaw or band saw away the waste.

Use a flush-trim bit to trim your disk even with the template. The extra template step does take more time and material, but you now have a disk for the next job, can make other templates from it, or use it over again to make a ring or smaller disk. You don't have to poke any holes in the work to use it, and there is no guesswork as to size and no risk to the work. Fifty cents worth of fiberboard goes a long way.

Figure 10-7

The thin web of MDF is all that remains between you and your disk. If you make your disk close to the dimension of your blank, you can start the jigsaw without drilling a hole. This web is also so thin you can break the disk out from the hole and just trim it clean with the PRC-TA 170 shown.

CHAPTER ELEVEN
The Mortising Jig

The mortise-and-tenon joint is one of the most important in cabinet- and furniture-grade situations. The joint is more commonly found in stick furniture (tables and chairs), but it can just as easily show up in paneled woodwork, such as bookcases, dressers and cabinets. The mortise can occur on the ends of a stick or anywhere in between, and on any face. In panels, the mortises are often found receiving tenons near the long-grain edges, but shelving can be tenoned anywhere, all the way across the grain from top to bottom.

MORTISE ANATOMY

There are three center lines to a mortise: One center line is midway in depth, and the other two are midway in length and width. A tenon

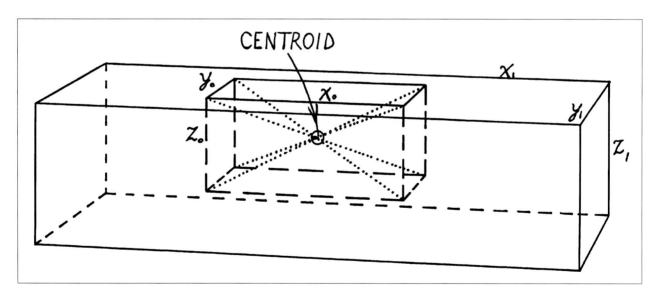

Figure 11-1

The centroid of the mortise is at the midlines of x, y and z. The centroid must lie on the center of the site you pick for it. It's easy enough to say and to lay out, but it's another matter to poke the hole in just the right place. The plunge router with its edge guides in tandem with the mortiser, and when properly adjusted, can excavate the mortise right where you want it.

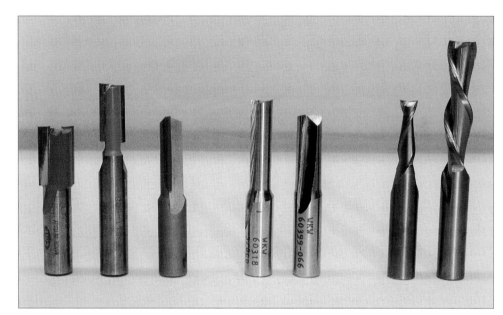

Figure 11-2
Any of these straight bits are capable of mortising. All solid-carbide cutters (the two on the far right) are ground to plunge straight into the stock. Some cutters are more efficient than others but even high-speed steel does a great job.

also has three center lines, but the nature of its function and shape have little to do with their creation or location. The positioning and the cutting of the mortise, on the other hand, are directly related to these center lines, and you must account for each one of them! The *z* axis (vertical depth of cut) is relatively easy to accommodate by plunging the cutter to the proper depth; it's of secondary importance. The center of the mortise (the intersection of the length and width center lines) can be located nearly anywhere on a workpiece, and herein lies half the adversity of mortising (Figure 11-1). The stick being mortised has three center lines of its own, and you have to line up the "cursors" so the mortise centroid (the intersection of its three axes) lands on the spot you've selected. Now, don't let the geometry scare you off. It's relatively easy to mortise the right-size excavation in the right place. I merely point all this out so you have a good definition of the problem before you let your router loose. Needless to say, you'll need a jig to help you position the mortise correctly and hold your work. Later on in this chapter I'll show you how to make the first evo-

lution of a jig, and one, I must point out, with enough flexibility built into it to take care of a lot of mortises in a lot of different places. But first, let's examine the mortising bit.

BITS FOR MORTISING

Mortising is possible only with straight bits. They can be spiral-ground, on-shear, straight up and down and of nearly any flute length. High-speed-steel, brazed-on-carbide and solid-carbide bits can all mortise equally well (Figure 11-2). The sides of the flutes always cut. Whether you hold the router still and push against the side of the mortise or sweep it down the length, they always cut.

The end of the cutter doesn't always cut, and this can be hazardous. Some of these cutters are pointed for boring right through the work; others are designed to cut a flat-bottom mortise (Figure 11-3). Ordinary straight bits cut on the bottom, but only if they're swept during and after the plunge. To plunge without sweeping the router (a not-so-easy maneuver) will present a risk, because the cutter will either burn up or

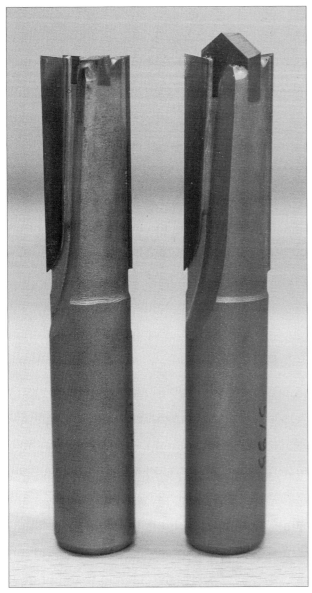

Figure 11-3
These two Wisconsin Knife Works cutters plunge straight through wood. The pointed boring end cutter is for through-stock plunging, and the other cutter is for blind flat-bottom work.

acceptable hazardous woodworking operations, and this is one I don't want my name associated with.

THE MORTISING FIXTURE

My mortiser (hereafter called a block mortiser because of its blocky, chunky appearance) has seen five or six evolutions and could still stand a few changes, but it's pretty good. The tool consolidates many of the important demands of the process. A plunge router and two edge guides are required to use the jig. One or both of the edge guides can be shop-made. The capacity in section (of a workpiece) is up to 1¾"-thick by 2⁵⁄₁₆"-wide by any length. You can mortise on any of the four faces of your work from end to end. If the capacity is under your requirements, I will point out the part and its dimension that needs changing to accommodate larger stock.

The block mortiser (Figures 11-4A, B, C) consists of an L-section block, which the work is clamped to and the router slides on top of; a clamp block, screwed to the body of the L-section block with three toggle clamps and tapped holes for three jack screws; an auxiliary hold-down block, either screwed or glued to the L-section block; and two sliding stops. The toggle clamps secure the work to the fixture. The jack screws raise the work level with the top of the block and prevent the work from being dislodged during the downward force of the plunge. And the hold-down block allows you an easy way to secure the jig (Figures 11-5, 11-6). As the router travels left and right, the long dimension of the mortise is defined. The sliding stops accommodate mortises to about 5½" long. The width of the mortise is controlled by the two edge guides.

find a spot (out of your control) where it can cut. This is especially challenging if you're cutting only one-cutter-diameter mortises. Router woodworkers worldwide cut mortises with non-plunging cutters, and you can learn to do it, too. However, there are, in my view, too many

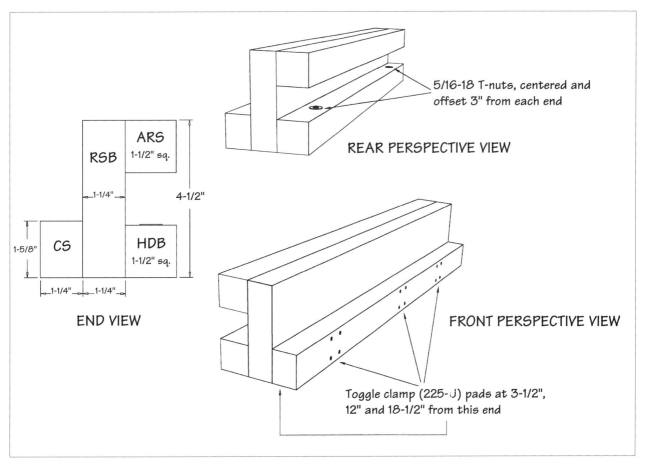

RSB

ARS
1-1/2" sq.

1-1/4"

4-1/2"

1-5/8"

CS

HDB
1-1/2" sq.

1-1/4"   1-1/4"

END VIEW

5/16-18 T-nuts, centered and offset 3" from each end

REAR PERSPECTIVE VIEW

FRONT PERSPECTIVE VIEW

Toggle clamp (225-J) pads at 3-1/2", 12" and 18-1/2" from this end

Figure 11-4A

Block mortiser: rear and front view oblique.

Figure 11-5
This is the back side of my mortiser. I've clamped it in place with two clamp knobs right through the bench.

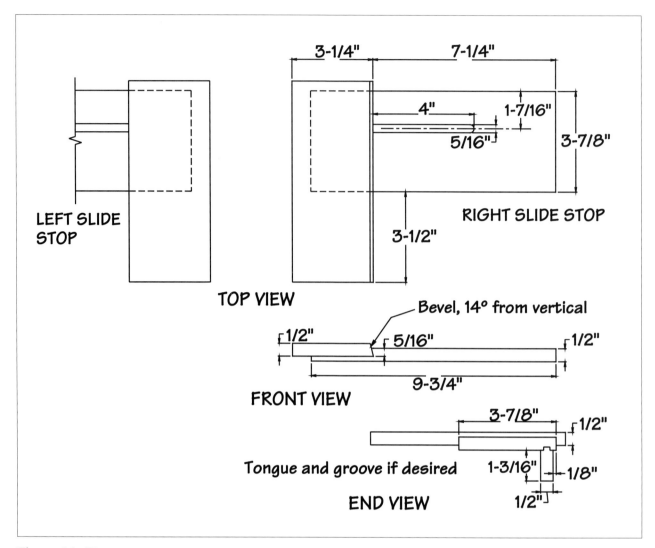

Figure 11-4B

Left- and right-handed stops.

ASSEMBLING THE MORTISING FIXTURE

The description that follows is for a screw-together assembly. Don't spend a lot of time on this first model; you will no doubt want to improve it as you gain experience. Make the second or third one better; use this one as an experiment.

STEP 1.   Cut and square up a 1¼"x4½"x24" piece of clear, straight-grained hardwood (oak, ash, walnut or beech, for instance). Add to the 4½" dimension as needed for a workpiece mortised (on the edge) over 3" (e.g., for work 3½" wide, add at least ⁹⁄₁₆" to this dimension). This is the router support block.

STEP 2.   Cut two pieces 1½"-square by 24". Install ⁵⁄₁₆-18 T-nuts in each piece, centered and 3½" from each end.

STEP 3.   Screw each piece flush top and bottom and on the same side of the router support block. The flanges of all the T-nuts must be facing each other. The piece on the top is for added router support and to accept the bolts that lock the travel of the stops. The bottom piece is the hold-down block that secures the jig. Use flathead #12 screws, and penetrate the router support block to about 1".

STEP 4.   Cut a 1¼"x1⅝"x24" clamp block. Add inch for inch to the 1¼" dimension for work over 1¾". Use three De-Sta-Co 225-U clamps on this piece to hold the work. Locate them on the 1⅝" face at 3½", 12" and 18½" from the left end. You may want to drill for a fourth clamp near the right end. I might use this clamp for added support on a workpiece that is to be end-mortised; at other times I clamp a stick under it for an index for the next workpiece (Figures 11-5, 11-6). Step 5 on page 103.

MORTISE CUTTER CHOICES

Nearly any straight bit can be used as a mortising tool, but you should consider the following when making the selection.

1. If you're cutting only one diameter, solid carbide should be a first choice. Almost all solid-carbide bits are plunging bits. The diameter selection is poor, but the length selection is good. They are very stiff, no matter what the diameter, and are less likely to break in severe service.

2. Use a shank length commensurate with your depth requirements. Don't try to reach greater depths by inserting only the minimum length of shank into the collet. Buy longer-shanked tools for deeper cuts.

3. Mortising is demanding work. Most of the work is being done on the bottom ⅜" of the tool. Short flutes with long shanks are better mortising tools than long flutes on short shanks because they cut better and they're less likely to break.

4. When cutting mortises greater than one cutter diameter, try to keep the cutter diameter to half or less of the mortise width. The more chopping room you give the cutter, the better.

5. Don't get overly concerned with flute design in your pursuit of selecting a cutter. Up-spiral cutters, for instance, aid in exhausting the chip from the mortise all right, but most of the time the clutter of the baseplate, casting or other contrivance will impede the escape of the chip anyway. Better that you stop cutting periodically and vacuum out the chip.

6. Don't shy away from high-speed steel. If you match the cut rate with the feed rate, you can cut a lot of mortises before resharpening. Consider Wisconsin Knife Works' HSS steel bits, as they have plunge ability. Production mortising, however, will require carbide.

7. Consider single-flute bits. Most are stiffer than two-flute bits, they plunge better, and you can line them up to the scribe lines easier.

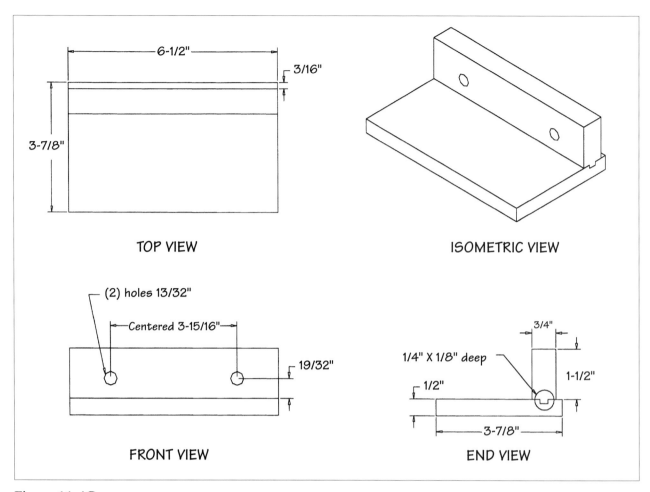

TOP VIEW

ISOMETRIC VIEW

(2) holes 13/32"

Centered 3-15/16"

19/32"

FRONT VIEW

6-1/2"

3/16"

3-7/8"

3/4"

1/4" X 1/8" deep

1/2"

1-1/2"

3-7/8"

END VIEW

Figure 11-4C

Edge guides for DeWalt 625.

Figure 11-6

This is the front side of the tool. The three jack screws penetrate the bench, then pass through threaded holes in the clamp block and support the work. The two steel bars that hold the plunger on the center clamp have been shortened for edge guide clearance.

Figure 11-7

The work edge of the stop must be 90° to the work. Check them with a machinist's square. The dimensions are scribed on the stop.

Figure 11-8

Handmade edge guides for the DeWalt 625 (also known as Elu 3338), shown here without a router for clarity. The dimensions scribed on the guide may or may not apply to your router, but at least you can use them for starters. The collars limit their position on the guide rods.

STEP 5.　Tap this piece or install ⁵⁄₁₆-18 T-nuts (flange up) 2" centered from each end and one in the center. Tap or drill through the 1¼" dimension. The ⁵⁄₁₆-18 thread is for the jack screws. These four pieces—the router support block, the added router support, the hold-down block and the clamp block—could be joined with tongue and groove joints for added squareness and registration. But the whole unit will be just as strong and work just as well with a bunch of #12 screws holding it together. Keep in

Figure 11-9

A scribe line on the center line of the maximum distance between the two slides (on the router support block) is a good starting point to line up with the center of the mortise on the work. A skinny workpiece was chosen here so you can see the jack screws in play.

mind that a 225-U toggle clamp can press to 500 pounds, so three of them exert a lot of tear-apart force on the jig. Use at least six screws to hold the clamp block in place.

STEP 6. Now make the stops. These, too, can be screwed together. Although mine look nice, they're not that great. Make yours out of two pieces, as shown in the drawing (Figure 11-4B). Just screw the pieces into an L-section. Cut an end-blinded ⁵⁄₁₆"-wide by 4"-long slot in each so the center of

the slot lines up with the center of the T-nut in the added router support. Once you have them sliding along nicely against the added router support, make sure the ends are 90° to the long edge of the router support block (Figure 11-7). Use ⁵⁄₁₆-10x2½" flathead machine screws and JFF 19305 flat-feet washers to secure the stops (Reid Tool Supply).

STEP 7. Jack screws and clamp knobs: Make the jack screws and clamp knobs from ⁵⁄₁₆-18 all thread. You will cut

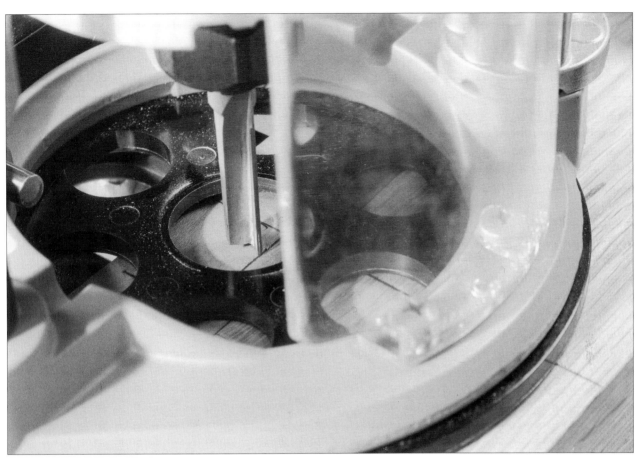

Figure 11-10

Single-flute bits, like this WKW 68422, plunge satisfactorily, and one flute is easier to line up with a scribe line than a two-fluted design.

Figure 11-11

For one-cutter-diameter mortises like this one, only one edge-guide setting is necessary. The Wedler Microfence simplifies this adjustment enormously.

the clamp-knob rods to a length to go through your bench and all the way through the hold-down-block T-nuts. Leave enough thread for a MPB-7 plastic clamp knob (Reid Tool Supply). Drill access holes in your bench for these clamp knobs. The jack screws should be 3" or 4" long. Their length is not critical. Use DK-131 knobs (Reid Tool Supply).

STEP 8.   Toggle clamps: Use three or four De-Sta-Co 225-U toggle clamps as suggested. The middle clamp will interfere with most edge guides, so you

Figure 11-12
With this mortise (more than one cutter diameter in width) two edge guides are in play.

Figure 11-13
This mortise is much wider than the cutter, so the router bit does some "swimming" before the guides come into play. The mortise on the left has not yet been resolved by the stops. The mortise on the right has been resolved. It always surprises me to see that the last 5 percent of the cut defines the outline of the whole thing. In single-diameter-cutter mortising there is no "freehanding" as the edge guide is always in play and the width of the mortise is evident from the first pass.

Figure 11-14
Once I've set up the coordinates for the mortise on my mortiser, I use a stop to locate the workpiece. Each subsequent workpiece is butted against the stop and held with at least two toggle clamps.

will have to hacksaw some of the spindle holder off to allow clearance (Figure 11-6). Use roundhead #10 or #12 sheet-metal screws to fasten the clamps to the clamp block.

STEP 9. Edge guides: The nicest way to mortise is with an edge guide up against the work and another one to slide against the edge of the added router support. Edge guides define the width of the mortise and aid in keeping the router flat on a relatively small surface. You'll need some long guide rods to attach a second edge guide to the opposite side of the casting. I made a pair of fancy guides, but you needn't go to such extremes. Most edge guides can be used on both sides of the router: Just get longer rods and buy a second guide, or make an L-section guide as shown (Figure 11-8). Drill the appropriate holes on the appropriate centers for your edge-guide rods. Secure the edge guide with two collars. (W.L. Fuller, Inc. sells collars with hundreds of hole sizes.)

You now have the makings for mortising, so square up some stock and lay out practice mortises.

USING THE BLOCK MORTISER

There are two fundamental ways of using the mortiser. One way assumes that you made your tenons to fit a mortise that is one cutter diameter in width; the other approach assumes that the mortises will be greater than a cutter diameter. A one-cutter-diameter mortise is much easier to set up for and cut, but it's very hard on the cutter and often not as cosmetically presentable as mortises greater than a single cutter diameter. The corners of a single-diameter-cut mortise are more difficult to chisel square, since the corner radii are usually harder to access and are larger. That aside, let's "cut to the chase."

Single-Cutter-Width Mortises

STEP 1.   Scribe the north and south boundaries and one edge of the mortise on the work.

STEP 2.   Set the toggle clamp spindles to the proper length and clamp the work in the jig so the long center line of the mortise is centered between the extremes of the sliding stops (Figure 11-9).

STEP 3.   Load up the router with the correct cutter and edge guides, and position the bit so it is tangential with the long scribe line (Figure 11-10).

STEP 4.   Position the cutter tangent to the inside of both the north and south cut lines and adjust the end stops (butt against the router base and lock).

STEP 5.   Set the plunge-router stops to cut as deep as your tenon is long. Start the motor, plunge, sweep and repeat to depth. Vacuum out the excavation from time to time, as there is really no easy way to get the chip out (Figure 11-11).

Mortising More Than One Cutter Diameter

You must lay out the entire perimeter for this mortise because the edge guides must be set for a slop. The slop is equal to the mortise width less one cutter diameter. Set the cutter tangent to all your scribe lines, and adjust the edge guides and stops so the cutter will stay within the confines of your lines (Figure 11-12).

Figure 11-15

I have band sawn into the interior of this mortise. The top half of the mortise was machined in the mortiser. Then I drilled the rest of the way through roughly on the drill press. I used the trimmer cutter on half the mortise from the opposite side, and I left some of it rough. The cutaway view is shown with the appropriate cutters.

Now plunge in the center of the mortise and waste away clockwise in the cavity. You will find that the cutter suffers most of its stress and strain in the center of the mortise where it is only cutting one diameter. As you approach the perimeter of the mortise, the cutter is taking less and less of a bite, and the walls of these mortises are therefore quite crisp (Figure 11-13).

To repeat the mortise on the next stick in the same place, merely index the work in the same place in the jig. You can position to a scribe line or butt the work against a stop. There is no need to lay out the mortises on subsequent pieces: The jig is already set up for all like mortises in equal-thickness material (Figure 11-14).

Deep Through Mortises

If you have a lot of mortises to do, waste away most of the mortise by drilling it out before routing. If your mortises are right through the stock, you can rout only half the way through, or as deep as is practical, and then drill out the remainder of the waste, staying inside the mortise confines. Working from the waste side of the mortise, rout the area clean with a flush-trimmer bit whose bearing is on the end of the cutter (Figure 11-15). Mortises through 3" or 4" stock are routable with this tactic.

Squaring the Corners or Rounding the Tenon

As you no doubt have discovered, the insertion of the tenon into the mortise is confounded by the round corners of the mortise. You can either round over the corners of your tenons or chisel out the corners of the mortise. Corner chisels are available for this, as are rasps and files to round over the tenons (Figure 11-16).

CHAPTER TWELVE
The Router Table Fence

Routers under 3½ hp are not to be compared to the 3- to 10-hp shapers from which they were derived. Don't expect to get shaper performance from a router table. While it is possible to get production quantities of some edge cuttings from router tables, in my view, it takes two routers to compete with one shaper (Figure 12-1). Versatility, not production output, is the real advantage of the router and router table.

Part of this versatility can be traced to the router fence. A fence can be as simple as a clamped-down stick or as complex as a Swiss Army Knife. This fence is somewhere between these extremes. A good fence will have a means for chip collection; a two-stage adjustment (rough and fine); a means of crowding the cutter (fences that move left and right); offset capability for full-thickness cuts such as jointing (Figure 12-2), made high enough to accommodate panels and such on edge; and a stop on the outfeed side for stopped cuts such as open mortises.

There are many low-tech and sophisticated

Figure 12-1
Both cutters cut the same profile but the shaper cutter will probably outlast the router bit by a factor of ten. The shaper has production as its advantage while the router table has versatility as its strength.

Figure 12-2
With an adjustable outfeed fence like this one, you can joint and profile in one pass (workpiece half-milled). This was, incidentally, the original intent of these cutters. Any cutter used on the router table that cuts full thickness can joint as well as profile in one pass.

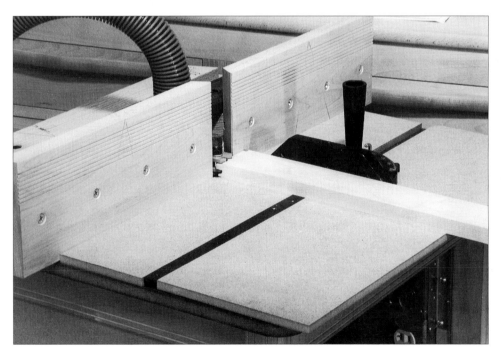

Figure 12-4
My miter gauge blade is sandwiched between two parallel pieces of MDF. This tactic keeps the blade parallel to the fence, simplifying adjustments. Use this setup for short end-of-stick cuts like coping and sticking.

ways to address these functions (Figure 12-4). Many inventors/manufacturers have addressed all of the critical control features of my fence and then some. Some of these designers have gone even further and embodied the positioning function—the most critical router fence responsibility—in specialized carriage systems for the router. Examples of these would be The Shop Center, Multi-Router and The Rout-R-Slide (Figure 12-5). Our sample will be simple: Slots, clamp bolts and a pivot will suffice for the mechanics, and MDF and wood instead of aluminum jig plate, phenolic and steel for the control surfaces (Figure 12-6A&B).

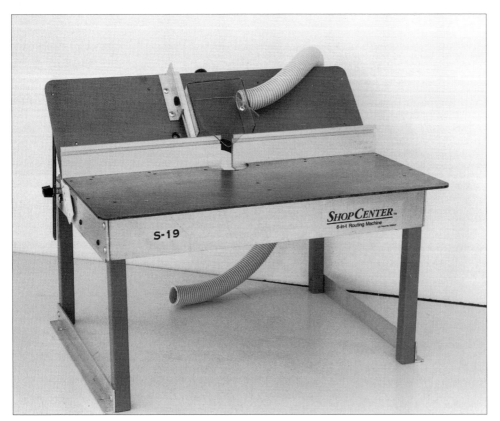

Figure 12-5
The Shop Center, in my view, has done the best job in consolidating the important features of table routing, and they've done it well. Photo supplied by the Shop Center.

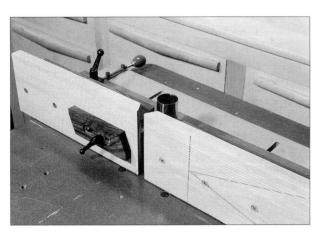

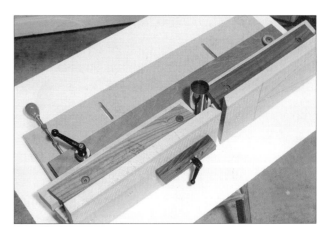

Figure 12-6A&B
My fence is some "distance" from the Shop Center but competitive nonetheless. Hardware and lumber will cost around $45.

THE FENCE DESIGN

The fence itself (two halves in T-section) is bolted to a common pivoting member, and the pivoting stick is bolted to a ¾"-thick piece of fiberboard (Figure 12-7). The fiberboard is slotted so that it can slide a few inches for the rough adjustment. The pivot allows about ½" of fine tuning at the center line of the cutter. Though modest, ½" of travel is adequate for most joinery, but perhaps is not enough if you use the fence (east/west) for multidepth work with large-diameter panel cutters. **Note:** Stage cuttings with very large diameter cutters should be done by raising the work up on a stack of ⅟₁₆" or ⅛" fiberboard panels, removing one for each pass.

Figure 12-7
In this view, you can see all the critical elements of the fence (rear view).

There are fewer surprises using this method since the cutter and fence are at full adjustment from the onset. Let's begin by cutting and machining each part of the fence and then doing the assembly.

The Fence Faces

The fence faces should not be made from discarded stock. They, and the rest of this assembly, should be culled from the best stock you have, so your router table won't be the genesis of a cascade of woodworking nightmares in the projects you make from it.

STEP 1.   Cut and mill two pieces of dry, straight-grained stock such as walnut, oak or maple to ⅞"x5"x13½" (Figure 12-8A). Bevel one end of each to 60° from the horizontal (Figure 12-9).

STEP 2.   Cut a ³⁄₁₆"-deep by ⅜"-wide slot on the back side of the faces, situated and centered 2³⁄₁₆" from the bottom.

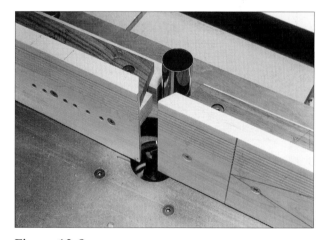

Figure 12-9
The beveled ends allow you to crowd the cutter more than if they were 90° cuts.

STEP 3.   Drill four ¼" holes and countersink as in the drawing.

STEP 4.   Drill and tap two pairs of ¼-20 holes on this same center line on the outfeed half of the fence. Each pair should be ⅞" apart, one set centered 2½" from the bevel-end and the other at 4½". These holes are for attaching the outfeed stop.

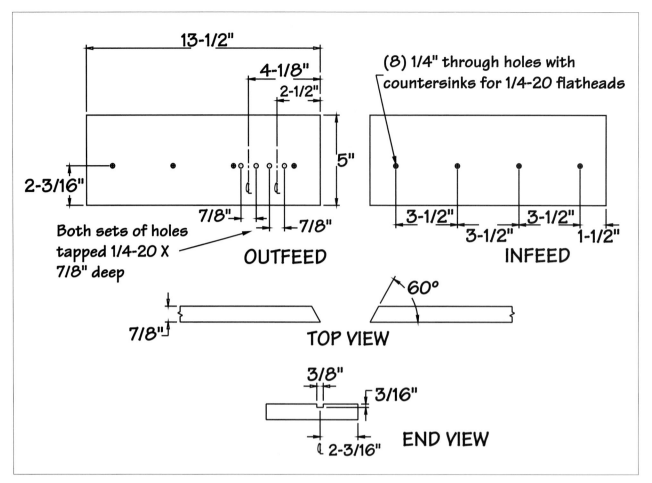

Figure 12-8A

Fence faces.

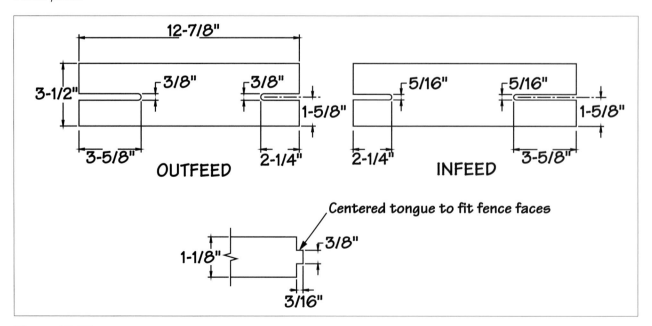

Figure 12-8B

Fence stiffeners.

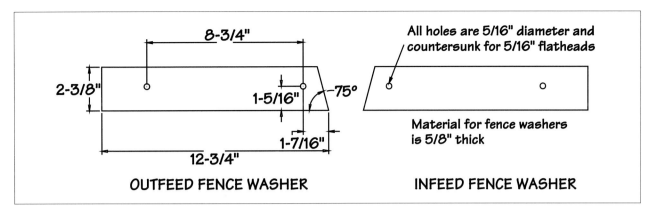

Figure 12-8C
Fence washers.

The Fence Stiffeners

These two sticks are tongued to fit the slots in the fence faces. They have the dual function of straightening the face and adjusting the halves left and right (Figure 12-8B).

STEP 1. Cut two pieces of hardwood to 1⅛"x3½"x12⅞" and tongue them to fit the faces.

STEP 2. Slot them as shown in the drawing, and register the end with the short slot in it even with the bevel. Indicate which face is up and to which half each belongs. Clamp the stiffener to the face board and transfer the screw-hole pattern to the tongue. Drill and tap for ¼-20x2" flatheads.

Fence Washers

The fence washers act just like the flat round doughnuts you're used to except these are made of hardwood. A washer like this (Figure 12-8C) keeps the clamp screws (two ⁵⁄₁₆-18x2½" flatheads) from boogering the stiffener and helps distribute the clamping force. Cut two pieces of ⅝"x2⅜"x12¾" hardwood, and bevel and drill as shown in the drawing.

PIVOTING MEMBER

The pivoting member receives the fence halves and pivots for the fine adjustment (Figure 12-8D). It also is the home for a vacuum tube that exhausts the chip right behind the cutter. It measures 1"x5⅜"x24½". There is a pivot hole in it and an arc-slot, ⁵⁄₁₆"x2", on a 20" radius.

STEP 1. Make the rectangle from hardwood or use 1" MDF. If you use MDF, use T-nuts for the fence assembly as threaded MDF may strip out. In hardwood, 1" of thread is very resistant to stripping. I'm using Jatoba, a very dense tropical hardwood, and I've actually broken a tap in it.

STEP 2. Drill a ⁵⁄₁₆" through hole for the pivot, and get out your circle-cutting subbase (chapter ten). Position the pivot arm for a 20" radius, and install a ⁵⁄₁₆" straight bit—solid carbide if you've got it—in the router. Cut about 2" to 2¼" of arc.

STEP 3. Locate the long center line of the plank and rout a space for the cutter.

STEP 4. Drill a 1½" hole for an exhaust tube centered and 2" from the edge. I use a 1½" vacuum hose on this tube with

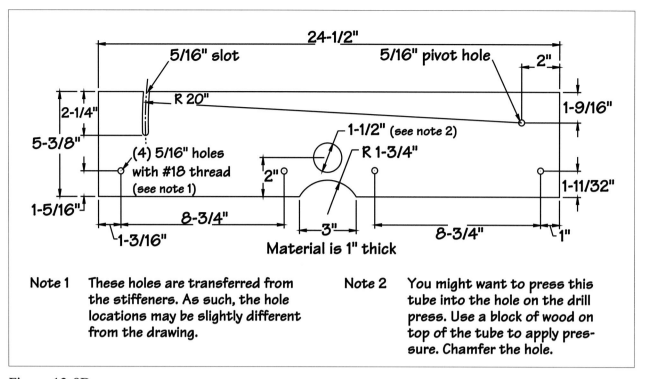

Figure 12-8D

Pivoting member.

variable results. When the cutter is close and well centered in the pocket, the chips are collected well. Often the cutter is not that well centered and the chip is blasted here and there. You might want to do some testing with the fence just clamped down on the router table to see if you can come up with a better collector before drilling this hole.

STEP 5.   Locate the holes for the fence halves as follows: Slide the outfeed half so the stiffener is tangent with the 1½" hole and the inside of the fence is about .020" to .025" away from the front edge of the pivoting member. This move allows you a little extra travel for offsetting the fence. Use the ⅜" transfer punch ½" from the inboard end of the slot for the slot

nearest the vacuum hole, and punch the other hole 1⅛" from the inboard end of its slot.

STEP 6.   Now position the infeed fence with its stiffener tangent to the right side of the 1½" hole and up against the pivoting member. Use a ⁵⁄₁₆" transfer punch and locate the bolt holes as previously.

THE CARRIER PANEL

The whole fence assembly is "carried" on a slab of ¾" MDF (Figure 12-8E). This panel will provide up to 4½" of rough travel with its 2¼" slots if you install two sets of ⁵⁄₁₆-18 T-nuts under your router table. The panel also serves as the host for two barrel nuts which in turn carry a 5½"-long ¼-20 bolt. This bolt is the screw that microadjusts the fence in and out. One rotation

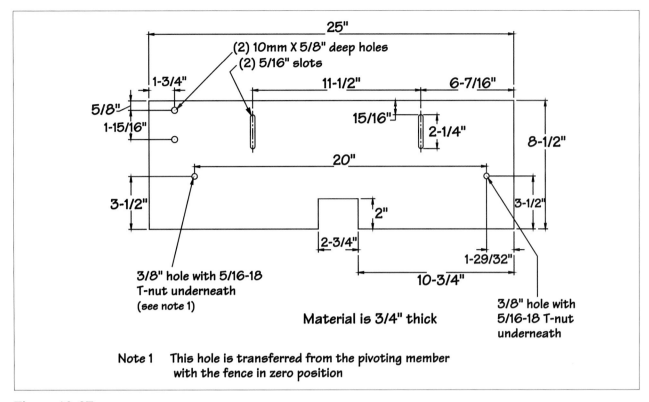

Figure 12-8E

Carrier panel.

of the screw moves the fence about .015" at the cutter (Figure 12-10).

STEP 1. Cut a ¾" piece of MDF into a 8½"x25" panel, and rout or saw a 2"x2¾" notch for the cutter as shown in the drawing.

STEP 2. Drill all the holes as shown, rout the two 2¼" slots on 11½" centers, and install the two T-nuts.

STEP 3. Make a 1"x2⅛"x20" washer (Figure 12-8F) to hold the whole affair secure. The holes in this piece are off-centered in width to accommodate the full range of fence positions.

STEP 4. Get a 5" hex ¼-20 carriage bolt, a Reid Tool ROA-4 threaded knob, and two #CD05 cross dowels from Bruss (see Sources). Also buy two

JFF-19305 steel washers (a.k.a. flat-feet), a KHB-68 lever, five ⁵⁄₁₆-18x2½" flat Allen socket drive screws, and a KHB-58 lever if you want one for the outfeed stop. The stud on the KHB-68 lever will need to be shortened ¹⁄₁₆", so hit that on the grinder before using it.

OUTFEED STOP

Cut a piece of ⁹⁄₁₆"-thick hardwood into a 10"x1⅞" rectangle, and through slot 4" of it. The slot should be ¼" wide followed by a ⅛"-deep by ¾"-wide counterbore (Figure 12-8G); chop to 7" long. The slot does not have to be centered. If not centered, you can get just as much use out of it as a longer one by turning it around. Ignore this triviality if desired.

Figure 12-10

An incremental fence position change can be made with any object of known thickness. A folded dollar, when placed between the pivoting member and the screw, will move the fence at the cutter by one dollar—a 50 percent return on your money!

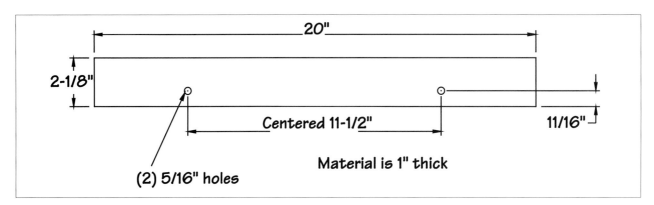

20"

2-1/8"

Centered 11-1/2"

11/16"

Material is 1" thick

(2) 5/16" holes

Figure 12-8F
Carrier panel washer.

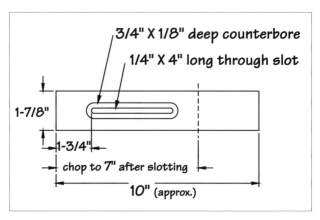

3/4" X 1/8" deep counterbore

1/4" X 4" long through slot

1-7/8"

1-3/4"

chop to 7" after slotting

10" (approx.)

Figure 12-8G
Outfeed fence stop.

Figure 12-11
A strong back clamped to the fence halves simplifies alignment. The Starrett straightedge verifies the straight line. Incidentally, a very straight fence requires your work to be very straight for best results.

ASSEMBLY

STEP 1. Sand, scrape and flatten the faces of the fences while screwed to their stiffeners. Hold them in your vise.

STEP 2. Clamp the MDF carriage down and put the screw and lever through the pivot board and tighten them. Press a length (3" to 4") of 1½" brass drainpipe into the 1½" hole.

STEP 3. Roughly position the fences for a 1"- to 1½"-diameter cutter. Now clamp a strong back (say a well-jointed 1"x3"x26" stick) across both fences. Tighten the four bolts through the two hardwood washers, and verify that the fences are in line (Figure 12-11).

STEP 4. Install the microadjusting bolt. You may want to put a flathead screw into the edge of the pivoting member where the adjuster strikes to keep the wood from wearing (Figure 12-12).

A FEW FENCE CUTS

Stopped-End Mortises

Stack as many ¼" panels as necessary to raise your work above the cutter. Set the appropriate outfeed stop for your work. Rout right to left removing a panel for each ¼" of depth (Figure 12-13).

The Fence for Tongues and Grooves

It makes no difference whether you cut the tongues or grooves first. For experience, cut them both ways, since there will be occasions when you may have to start with either a groove or a tongue. A ³⁄₁₆" side-to-side (lateral) depth of cut is typical, so let's start by making a tongue ³⁄₁₆" wide, one-third the thickness of the stock. We'll use 1"-thick material.

Figure 12-12
The screw may wear a step into the edge of the fence carrier if a strike plate is not present. Countersink a cap screw into the edge where the screw makes contact.

Figure 12-13
The most expeditious way to change depth of cut on the router table is by stacking panels under the work. The open mortise is 1" deep.

STEP 1.　Collet up a rabbet bit or a ⅝"-diameter or larger straight bit.

STEP 2.　Set the vertical depth of cut. It is not critical, but keep it as close to one-third the thickness as is practical (²¹⁄₆₄" to ¹¹⁄₃₂").

STEP 3.　Adjust the fence to take about ³⁄₁₆" of stock. Again, this depth of cut is not critical.

STEP 4.　Now rabbet all the boards requiring tongues on both faces (Figure 12-14), producing centered tongues. The tongues should be around .333", or a nominal ¹¹⁄₃₂"-thick by ³⁄₁₆"-wide.

STEP 5.　Select a slotter that is thinner than the tongue but whose thickness, doubled, is greater than that of the tongue. This ensures that the vertical depth needn't be changed to produce the correct slot. A ³⁄₁₆" slotter will do. Remember: One machine setting for either or both sexes of the joint will simplify the process enormously.

STEP 6.　Collet up the cutter and set the fence

Figure 12-14
The fence is set to allow about ³⁄₁₆" depth of cut. The cutter height is about one-third the height of the workpiece. Dividing the work into two passes like this (one rabbet per side) is easier on the cutter and the cuts are usually pretty clean and free of tear-out. Note the absence of an end-bearing.

to cut less than the tongue width. Adjust the height of the cutter so that the bottom of a cutter tooth is parallel with the bottom of the tongue cut in step 3 (Figure 12-15).

STEP 7.   Cut a slot on the edge of equal-thickness scrap material. Turn the board over, changing nothing, and repeat the cut (Figure 12-16). Check for a slip fit. Adjust the cutter up or down until a slip fit is achieved.

STEP 8.   On the same piece of scrap, continue slotting (both faces) while changing the fence setting until the shoulders of the tongue just "kiss" the edge of the slotted piece of scrap (Figure 12-17). Once that condition is met, increase the fence setting so the slot width is deepened by about the thickness of a dollar bill and slot all your stock, passing the cutter with the face side up and the face side down. This completes the joint.

Figure 12-15
Set a tooth of the slotter to a depth that is parallel to the bottom of the tongue.

Figure 12-16
Obviously the tongue has a long way to go before its shoulders reach the edge of the slotted workpiece. The fit in thickness is correct, however. I've slotted only a few inches of the "calibration" stick.

Figure 12-17
The depth of cut is correct now. All the surfaces meet up smartly.

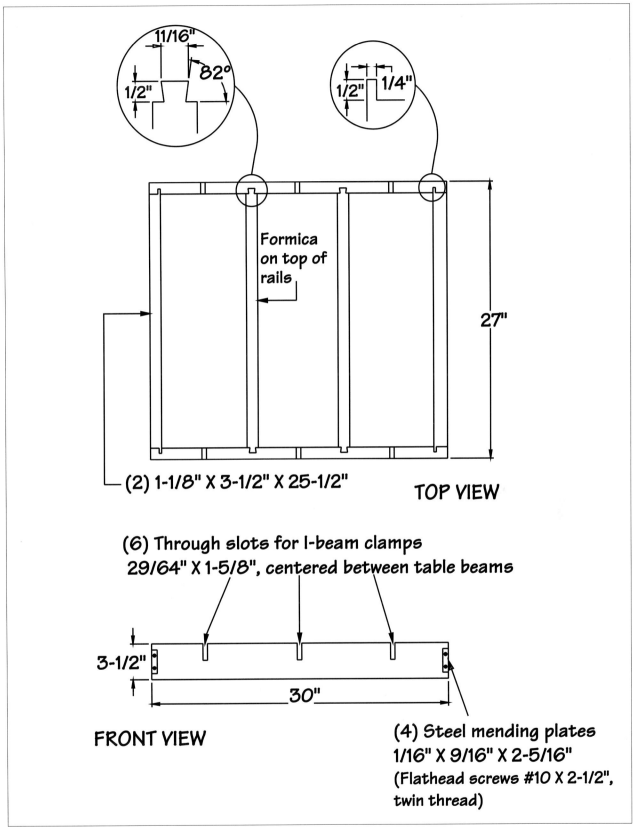

11/16"

82°

1/2"

1/2"   1/4"

Formica
on top of
rails

27"

(2) 1-1/8" X 3-1/2" X 25-1/2"

TOP VIEW

(6) Through slots for I-beam clamps
29/64" X 1-5/8", centered between table beams

3-1/2"

30"

FRONT VIEW

(4) Steel mending plates
1/16" X 9/16" X 2-5/16"
(Flathead screws #10 X 2-1/2",
twin thread)

Figure 12-19
The press frame.

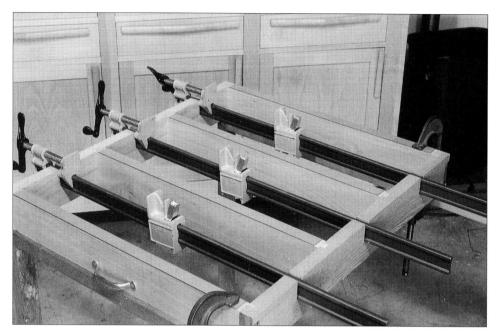

Figure 12-18
*The four beams are in
the same plane, so the
work starts out flat
from here.*

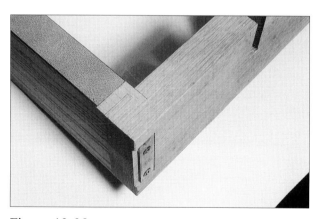

Figure 12-20
*This offset joint is adequate for this connection
because it's reinforced with screws. The surfaces of
the beams are covered with Formica to keep the
glue from sticking.*

GLUING UP A TONGUE AND GROOVE PANEL

Flat wood and a well-articulated tongue and
groove joint do not guarantee a perfect panel.
You still need to assemble them, and they should
be assembled on a flat surface. What follows is
the description of a simple frame to hold your
clamps (in my case, Jorgensen 7230s) and press
your work flat while the glue goes to work.

The Press Frame

This press frame is designed for panels to about
20"-wide by 40"-long, though I have glued larger panels in it (Figures 12-18, 12-19). The frame
holds three Jorgensen 7230 I-beam clamps. Add
10" for each additional clamp and inch for inch
in depth for every inch greater than 20" in
desired panel width. My press is held together
with sliding dovetails and tongues and grooves.
Shallow tongue and groove joints are also
acceptable, but you should use some screws
through the end grain if your joints are shallow
(Figure 12-20).

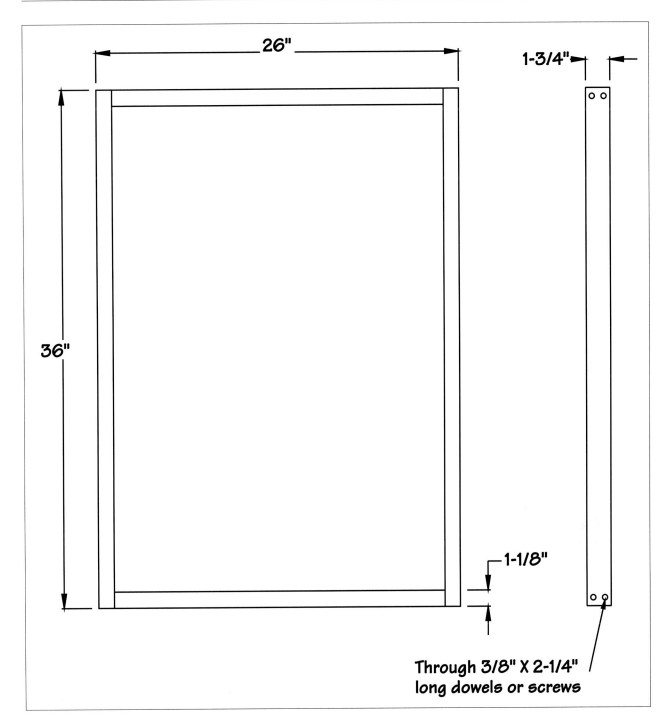

26"

36"

1-3/4"

1-1/8"

Through 3/8" X 2-1/4" long dowels or screws

Figure 12-21
Sketch of stand for press frame.

Figure 12-22

These I-beam clamps can press up to 2000 pounds each, so three clamps equals 6000 pounds! The panel will cup without these hold-down clamps and cauls.

STEP 1.   Cut four pieces of 1⅛"x3½"x25½" hardwood.

STEP 2.   Cut a single-faced ¼"-wide by ½"-long tenon on both ends of two of the sticks and ¹¹⁄₁₆"-wide by ½"-long dovetail (8°) tenons on the ends of both center sticks (use Jesada 618-674 or equivalent dovetail bit). Substitute shallow (say, ³⁄₁₆"x⅝" wide) stub tenons if desired.

STEP 3.   Cut mortises to receive tenons.

STEP 4.   Notch or plow six blind slots as shown in the drawing ²⁹⁄₆₄"-wide by 1⅛"-long. Narrower slots will jam the I-beams, wider ones are OK, but ½" should be your maximum.

STEP 5.   Assemble and cover the four cross beams with strips of Formica.

STEP 6.   Make two stands to support the press frame. Make them from 1⅛"x1¾" material. There is nothing special about these frames. 2x4s and nails will work (Figure 12-21).

Gluing Up

Attach the press frame to the stands using C-clamps and place the three clamps in the slots. Sort your boards, and apply a uniform bead of glue to the corners of the tongue and groove joints and along the center lines of shoulders and tongues if time permits. Place your glue up in the press frame and lightly squeeze out the excess glue. Clean up the glue with a scraper and wet rags (for vinyl glues). Loosen the clamps and turn the assembly over and clean the glue from this face. Now clamp the work down (Figure 12-22) on to the beams and squeeze with the I-beam clamps until the glue line closes. Panels from a press like this are always flat. To keep them flat, sticker them between operations.

SOURCES

Adjustable Clamp Co.
417 N. Ashland Ave.
Chicago, IL 60622-6397
Excellent source for all sorts of clamps.

Amana Tool Corp.
120 Carolyn Blvd.
Farmingdale, NY 11735
(800) 445-0077
A huge selection of wonderful router bits.

Bridge City Tool Works
1104 NE 28th Ave.
Portland, OR 97232
(800) 253-3332
Precision layout and metrology tools.

Bruss Fasteners
P.O. Box 88307
Grand Rapids, MI 49518-0307
(800) 563-0009
Hardware and other specialty fasteners.

De-Sta-Co
P.O. Box 2800
Troy, MI 48007
The source for toggle clamps.

DeWalt Industrial Tool Co.
P.O. Box 158
625 Hanover Pike
Hampstead, MD 21074
(800) 4-DeWalt
Electric hand tools and offset router subbases.

Eagle America
P.O. Box 1099
Chardon, OH 44024
One of the largest router bit selections.

Fine Woodworking Magazine
63 S. Main St.
Newtown, CT 06470
A rich source of state-of-the-art woodworking.

J&L Industrial Supply
31800 Industrial Rd.
Livonia, MI 48150
(800) 521-9520
Ground straightedges.

Jesada Tools, Inc.
310 Mears Blvd.
Oldsmar, FL 34677
(813) 891-6160
Premier router bits and router offset subbases.

Microfence
11100 Cumpston St. #35
North Hollywood, CA 91601
(800) 480-6427
Edge guides and circle cutter pivots.

Paso Robles Carbide, Inc.
731-C Paso Robles St.
Paso Robles, CA 93446
(805) 238-6144
Router bits, including many of the extreme sizes.

Patrick Warner
1427 Kenora St.
Escondido, CA 92027
(760) 747-2623; fax (760) 745-1753
E-mail: pat@patwarner.com
Web site: www.patwarner.com
Maker of acrylic offset subbases.

Popular Woodworking Magazine
1507 Dana Ave.
Cincinnati, OH 45207
(513) 531-2690
Web site: www.popwood.com

Porter-Cable Corp.
P.O. Box 2468
Jackson, TN 38302
(901) 668-8600
Routers, accessories and electric hand tools.

Reid Tool Supply Co.
2265 Black Creek Rd.
Muskegon, MI 49444-2684
(800) 253-0421
Jig and fixture hardware of all sorts.

Ridge Carbide Tool Co.
595 New York Ave.
Lyndhurst, NJ 07071
(800) 443-0992
Sharpening of router bits.

Rockler (The Woodworkers' Store)
4365 Willow Dr.
Medina, MN 55340
(800) 279-4441
Many products, including offset router subbases.

The L.S. Starrett Co.
121 Crescent St.
Athol, MA 01331
Precision scales, calipers and layout tools, etc.

Ken Schroeder
3120 Gaewood Ct.
Alliance, OH 44601
(330) 821-7571
Photographic printing service and consulting.

Whiteside Machine Co.
4506 Shook Rd.
Claremont, NC 28610
(800) 225-3982
Very competitive router bits; all American made.

Wisconsin Knife Works
2505 Kennedy Dr.
Beloit, WI 53511
(608) 363-7888
Plunging and other router bits.

W.L. Fuller, Inc.
P.O. Box 8767
7 Cypress St.
Warwick, RI 02888
(401) 467-2900
Router bits, drilling tools.

Wolfcraft, Inc.
P.O. Box 687
1222 W. Ardmore Ave.
Itasca, IL 60143
(630) 773-4777
Nice spring clamp for temporary holdfast and many other tools.

Wood Magazine
1912 Grand Ave.
Des Moines, Iowa 50309

Woodhaven
5323 W. Kimberly Rd.
Davenport, IA 52806
(800) 344-6657
Routing equipment.

Woodwork
P.O. Box 1529
Ross, CA 94957-9987
A magazine for all woodworkers.